NAKED TRUTH

Diary of a Glamour Model

BY
VICKI REBECCA

Published by Vicki Rebecca Publishing
www.vickirebecca.com

With all the lots of joy
to Grace Revell
from Vicki Rebecca
xxx

Note From the Author

Naked Truth: Diary of a Glamour Model is MY story, a large part of which took place in the 1970s and 1980s when language that is considered derogatory today was not recognised in that way. As a therapist I am fully behind the recognition of that which causes feeling less than or causes trauma. However, I also believe in authenticity. It is for that reason, that despite current realisations, I decided to stay true to how it was. I believe it best portrays the background of my life. I have been brutally honest in this book and the person I expose most is myself. I do so to open doors to the future. We are not our past, yet the past is part of what forms us, and so for me it is important to report it as it was to the best of my ability without overusing the editorial pen to assure some false popularity.

Dedication

I wrote this book with my mother in my heart and with my daughter by my side. I publish it for the grandchildren yet to be born—know we are behind you, that we love you and our dream is for the new story we know you will weave into existence.

Disclaimer

This work depicts actual events in the life of the author as truthfully as recollection permits and/or can be verified by research. Occasionally, dialogue consistent with the character or nature of the person speaking has been supplemented. All persons within are actual individuals; there are no composite characters. The names of most individuals have been changed to respect their privacy.

Contents

Prologue

I knew I wouldn't see Harry. This time, I'd made sure of it. Drawn the final curtain. We weren't man and wife any longer. I wasn't his bottle of beer now, nor his jacket, I could even smile at a handsome waiter if I wanted to. Yet I reminisced about our time together during the whole journey: the drive to Stonehaven, the train ride to Haymarket. I even wondered if he'd ever sit on the double-decker that took me to Edinburgh Airport. I remembered it how it used to be, expectation flooding my body as I navigated the fluorescent-lit arrival halls, bought my visa, grabbed my bags and the final wearisome wait as the evening heat washed over me.

Then, just as I'd start to wonder if he was coming: 'Hello stupid!'—I'd hear that voice, catch a wink; a kiss, cautious, but enough to let me smell his warmth, the faint whiff of cigarette smoke, and to feel the body memories of us. With a cheeky grin he'd hurry me along to whatever beat-up car he'd managed to borrow, and with my heart leaping into my throat we were off on our adventure—

This time, the only fragrance was the delicate orange blossom of spring.

Why I chose the damp chill of Scotland over that, I'll never know. I asked my driver to pull in at the petrol station: 'Red Marlboro and a Coke,' I said, pointing. The Coke was always full fat, and that was exactly what I wanted. I sat at the metal bistro table out front allowing my resting eyes to enjoy the blur of the traffic whizzing by, my ears to acclimatise to the now familiar tongue as my driver passed time with the vendor, leaving me to my quiet reverie. I crossed my legs, lit up, took a couple of deep drags of the acrid smoke, then chased it with the forbidden Coke on its cleansing journey down my throat. Scanning the road one last time over the rim of the bottle, I called to my driver: '*Haydi gidelim!*' Let's go!—a reunion awaited!

Lahli, sitting in the foyer, was from Essex. We'd met three years before on a yoga holiday, just before I met Harry. She leapt up to catch my attention: 'Dahling, you look gorgeous as eva'!' she cooed, greeting me with a warm squeeze; then as we collapsed into the luxe sofa she giggled. 'Hilarious, hon, just as I spotted you coming in with your big, bouncy, beautiful blonde hair, clingy leather pants and your red lipstick, all the male heads were blatantly turning as if to catch us in an incestuous sex sandwich. It's just like, "*There she is, this is what she does when she arrives in Turkey, halts all the male conversations!'"* We laughed. 'Let's get you a drink,' Lahli suggested.

'Ooh I'd love a crisp white; what a fucking journey I've had, been downing Marlboro and full fat Coke, I just needed a little something.'

Lahli giggled as we moseyed up to the bar. 'Oh well, you know what, hon, if you fancy a little something else there's a couple of guys downstairs.' Then checking that the couple along the bar from us couldn't hear, she stage-whispered. 'Reckon they were faffing around with her in the red, I could hear her moaning and groaning—*uh, oh, ahhhhhhhh*—must be like the best friggin' massage on the planet!' She squealed. Then straightening up she said, 'They obviously got the Indian vibe from me, which is like, "Don't even touch me wiv a samosa, cos you ain't getting nuffink." Anyway, if you feel like it, I'm sure they'd be happy to give you a finger of fudge or anything else you fancy.'

We were both giggling when the manager arrived fishing rod swinging, and got straight into VIPing me, sending staff members scurrying to help with my luggage, and booking me in for that 10 p.m. massage. We sent him off with a promise to join him for lunch the next day, sipped our drinks and sallied downstairs. Lahli had a conditioning treatment while I, naturally, had my massage, and suitably chilled we began the important job of making plans for the rest of our trip.

Later, lying in the hotel's white cotton bed surrounded by the colourful contents of my luggage, which I'd flung around the room in search of my toothbrush and valerian, I was intermittently exchanging angry texts with Harry:

You come here.

No, you come here, lazy ass.

I tried to remain aloof, unavailable, the bloody Ice Queen—though I did wonder if I was having a belated midlife crisis. They say that fifty is the new forty and I looked young for my fifty-nine years. No sagging, squashed-together tits. No thick, old-lady crocodile skin …

Truth is, I had a nervousness about me that whole trip, maybe even longer, a crazy kind of wildness—I still can't work out exactly what it was all about. I loved Harry. It was my one and only relationship where I stayed right in the moment and accepted him totally, unconditionally, exactly as the six-orgasms-a-night never-any-money cocksure gigolo prick wanker he was. It was the very best relationship I'd ever had, and incredibly the easiest to let go. The texts, well, they were mere lip service, perhaps, a wondering out loud, but we had let it go, broke it off, ended it, moved on.

It was while I was with Harry that I finished writing my first book. That was when Robert told me to take out the preface and use it to start my autobiography, *this* book. Robert was the guy who told me I hadn't dug deep enough. Nosy bastard was right, I knew it, and I also knew I wasn't ready. Looking back, it seems, somehow that conversation was an activation, an intention setting. It also scared me. I remember worrying about how others would receive such a book, about how I could align some of my now beliefs with my past behaviours. I thought a lot about that, about what role models were available to us as women, and how on earth we could set our trajectory in a boy's world, where everything was calculated using a boy's measuring stick, a world where even the Creator was a him. What was needed was a new language to talk about these things, some conversation that didn't channel just our inner bitch, something more than another devastatingly doomed quest for self-improvement where we could unlock events we've kept secret, no matter how hideous, where we could look at the past without shame or humiliation, and just *remember* ...

The realisation hit me the next day, as Lahli and I strolled through the hotel after our morning spa to check out the pool and tennis courts before lunch. I can't to this day remember what led to the conversation—I only remember the look of utter shock and horror on dear sweet Lahli's face when I spluttered it out.

'You wot?!' She stopped in her tracks, hands gripping mine, mascaraed eyes flooding with tears. '*Wot* happened? … *Wot* did your mum say? … You didn't tell no one? … Vicki, wot the fuck! Where *were* people?' Her shocked face told me all the emotions I ought to have felt, and somehow didn't …

CHAPTER ONE

The Graveyard

Leaning back on a gravestone, his weight propped on one elbow, the other resting on his thigh, a blade of grass twirling between his fingers, he watched. Her curly hair bounced with each step: navy blue blazer, white shirt, high school tie, short, pleated skirt, white tights and round-toe sandals. He called out to her: 'Fancy gan' for a wak?' She turned her head; she hadn't expected to find him alone inside the graveyard. Taking it in, she stood staring at him. With his skinhead, braces, and swagger, he was cheeky and charming, shiny cock, warm lips, nice smell. The smartest, most-pressed Ben Sherman in town. Pale blue turn-ups and polished bovver boots. She fancied him and wanted to be his special girl. She'd experimented with sex before, but he was the first to give her a proper fucking. She bled and was wet after. It was down at the Denburn, one of the places where people got fucked in Aberdeen. Denburn, Broad Hill, Torry Battery. Underage girls, confused transsexuals, and anyone else who didn't cause too much trouble.

The sun made his blue eyes twinkle as he beckoned her over, and when he kissed her, she realised he really liked her and wanted her to be his girl. 'I've got a car, ye comin'?' She thought she was Ali MacGraw from *Love Story,* and was walking on air as he led her by the hand out of the graveyard through the side gate and on to Back Wynd. Proper acknowledgement. But wait, was that his mates standing by the car? Her heart sinking, she looked up at him; she'd thought they were going to be alone. 'We'll jist gi' them a lift,' he whispered. She felt nervous from the minute she climbed into the Wolseley with them. Why didn't she just turn away? After a few minutes' drive, he said, 'We're jist gan in here for a fag.'

They all shoved out, and she got in the back seat with him. Scared at first, she struggled a little; his mates were outside, watching and giggling, but his kisses made her forget, so it was good. He finished and the mate he'd called Freddy appeared at the door.

'No!'

'It's jist Freddy, he's a'right.'

'*No!*' Scraping her heels on the Wolseley leather, scrambling to get her pants up and trying to get off her back at the same time. No chance, Freddy was right on top of her. Older, harder, smellier. Wiry jaw cutting into her neck. Freddy was a fighter with a reputation for violence; he was inside her in seconds, she was already wet. She froze. She let him. In that exact moment, at age fourteen, she knew what they had done. She also knew there was no point in saying no. Fear, regret, and inevitability. Rape. It was quick.

Then the sinking feeling of terror when she realised: *That wasn't it, there was more, the unthinkable was going to happen.* She knew what was next; they did too, they held her. Her scream brought a slap; she took it and shut up. His scar-filled, cross-eyed face imprinted on her mind forever. Guts churning, despising the body she lived in.

They left her there. She checked herself all over, messy, yet how would anyone really know what had happened? Still wondering what the world might think if they saw her, she walked down those long stairs from Upperkirkgate to where Morrison's is today, crossed the road and found a phone box in East North Street. Cathy and her brother didn't take too long. Cathy looked her up and down, taking in her dirty, torn white tights, and said with a laugh of disgust:

'Fit the fuck hiv you bin deein'?'

'Johnny Ross an' 'em jist gang-banged mi.'

'Ye fuckin' cow.'

That was that.

* * *

She didn't go out for a long, long time. When she did, she was hypervigilant. Scanning for the large, scarred white face, the one that made her feel like vomiting. She ran in the opposite direction every time she saw him. When he showed up at the Beach Ballroom on a Saturday night, she'd leave instantly through the back door. One night he must have spotted her too; she ran into the dark, through the rough ground, over the Broad Hill, up the dimly lit streets beyond and into the pitch-black graveyard where she hid until she sensed that the coast was clear.

Once they'd got you, she knew you could become marked, something to be used, frozen in your own shame. She understood that, and she wouldn't let that be her story; although her young head didn't quite put it all together, she didn't realise she could choose to stay away from these people. It simply didn't cross her mind. She wanted to be part of it. To belong. For that, she paid the price of swallowing the stinking shame, the violence, and the rage. She kept her innocence on the inside as she braced against the damage done. The loss of soul.

She hung around downtown, snarled, smoked, chewed gum. The women hated her with a mixture of contempt and jealousy. The beginning of a lifetime of not feeling enough: wrong, dirty, damaged. Finally, she couldn't stand it. Without a backward glance, no fear, no thought of safety, no recriminations, with her short curls, faded Levi's, and the Who's 'I'm Free' playing in her head, the girl named Vicki took to the road.

CHAPTER TWO

The Road (Vicki's Story)

And so, with Roger Daltrey's scream echoing in my ears, as 1970 dawned I began running. Running away from home. From Aberdeen. From the abuse and the fuckings. Running to catch up with my dreams.

My thoughts were on this wonderful life I'd create for myself in London, working in a boutique, walking on the King's Road, shopping, and going out with my boyfriend, a boyfriend just like the one I'd dream of after reading *Jackie*, my favourite teen comic book.

That life was the dream.

The truth was I ended up back home every single time. Maybe the sweet station master at Victoria told the bobby on the beat where he could pick me up. Indeed, any bobby worth his salt could see me sticking out like a sore thumb. To the lorry cab drivers and the truckers in the greasy Joe cafes on the road, I was jailbait.

I returned to face a bitter unhappiness at home. I wasn't sure why and concluded there was something wrong with me. I'd been told enough times I was a problem child. The kids at my posh school hated me because I wasn't posh. The kids round the doors hated me because I *went* to a posh school. In the end, I hated myself. I was hell-bent on destruction and would do anything to ease the pain. Shoplifting was one of my many pranks, mostly done for a laugh—but the fighting, that was something else. I didn't understand the rage and fury that built up inside of me, built up to the point that when the valve needed to open, to release all that anguish and pain, someone was going to get it.

Someone turned out to be Mary Brown.

As a punishment for misbehaving during the week, instead of getting to sleep at my grandma's and get out on Saturday night, Mum and Dad would drag me out to our caravan in the tiny country village of Ballater. After one such weekend, I returned to school on Monday to have whispered in my ear: 'Mary Brown shagged Gary up the Broad Hill on Saturday night!' I'd been seeing Gary—everybody knew. The whisperer—Mary's arch-rival, Linda McBain—had the whole school primed for a fight, waiting to see what I'd do. I pummelled Mary and cut her eye badly; the school took it seriously and the police were called.

However, I didn't expect them to come back to question me a second time. After all, they already had all the details of the fight; but wait, they said something about if that cut eye had been some fragment of an inch closer to her eye, the charge would have been more serious. Had something happened? No, nothing like that! They wanted to know if I had sex with Gary Stewart?! I held my head down so that my eyes could make a thousand rotations around my brain away from their gaze, while my mind frantically wondered how they could possibly know I had sex, and why would they be interested? I was a kid. They also asked if Mary had sex with him. My brain responded at last: as I jumped on her I called out: 'Ya slag!' What a door those two words had opened!

At least, so I believed at the time.

Next time I was down at the graveyard, Johnny told me to say that I'd slept with lots of boys, and that the first one I slept with was someone my same age. It hurt that he wanted me to say I'd been with so many boys, but that was the hidden part of me. The part I pushed to the surface was the tough girl who knew how to handle the pigs. Primed and prepared, north wind blowing in my face, I walked up Cairncry Road to the police box at the top of the hill, and that's what I said. I did as Johnny asked and gave the policeman a list of names. They flew out of my mouth like dry vomit. They knew; I could feel the cold steel of a policeman faced with a liar. They informed me that I'd have to have a virginity test. I guessed that was the punishment; why else would they need proof of something I had already admitted? I simply accepted it as 'How they did it' and that it was what I deserved.

An appointment was made in a clinic in Aberdeen's West End. Big posh houses not far from my big posh school. My probation officer told my mum and dad that they could only give the test with their permission. I pleaded with them. My dad left, shoulders hunched in despair and anger. He refused to have anything more to do with it. Unbelievably, my mum stayed. My mother had always been the soft one; I could dominate her easily. I remember as an infant realising what a soft touch she was and being both elated at the potential of manipulating her and bitterly disappointed at her weakness. In the face of my father's overly Victorian attitude, she was the voice of reason; Mum always tried her best to persuade Dad to let me out when he tried to keep me in. And here was my dad walking away and her staying!

She gave consent. I sat in the bay window of that waiting room: the glossy magazines gazing up at me, the smell of dust, and the slightly worn carpets, a bit like my gran's dark red one. It was so hard to push the words out: 'Please don't make them examine me like that, Mum!' and then to receive her childish, guarded refusal in return. It was baffling, yet a betrayal I expected. I could feel her passive-aggressive grasp of power, and wondered what the hell? What shame from the recesses of her mind was I paying for here?

My thoughts were broken as my probation officer walked into the room. He took me across the hallway to the examination room and explained that if I didn't cooperate, I would be restrained because they had my mother's consent. He allowed me one more shot at persuading her. I cried, begging my mother, 'Please don't make me go through this, Mum! I'll never forgive you if you let them do this to me!' She turned her head away and looked out the window. Shame and disgust for who knows what resting on those shoulders. She turned her back on me that day.

That took a lifetime to forgive.

I had no option but to be raped again. I walked back alone. My probation officer opened the door for me; I looked at him. 'I'm telling you, I'm not a virgin, why do they have to do this?' There was one lady police officer and two policemen; all three were in uniform, there to hold me down, but I made no struggle as the doctor gave me an internal examination to confirm the absence of a hymen, an absence that had never been denied.

As far as I know, no charges have ever been brought against anyone on that list.

Afterwards, things were bitter at home, culminating in me and my dad having a punch-up in the local shopping centre when I tried to break a milk bottle over his head when he came to drag me home. I got sent to a council home, Broomhell Hostel, a big old mansion southwest of the city centre. The room was all right, located on the first floor with a huge bay window. The other single bed, although it shared a wall with mine, was far enough away. Who was my roommate? Who was in the other bed? She returned the next night. Her name was Dot. She spat her name out like an assault, daring me to challenge that she was the one and only Dot. I got it. Dot was not quite sixteen, but to me she was a woman already, with milk-bottle white skin, short-cropped red hair, a sharp nose, and a hardened face. Glaswegian. 'I wiz expelled frae borstal an' they cannae find an approved school that'll tak' me,' she said with pride. Officially known as List D schools, in an attempt to soften the label for housing for the nation's young criminals—borstal! This was apparently where I was going next. I took Dot's statement with a pinch of salt; surely if she was that bad, she would be sent to jail. As if reading my mind, she interjected: 'Aye, they'll maybe send me tae the jail on ma sixteenth.' Exaggeration or not, Dot was a different animal to me, and I knew in that moment that I could end up behind bars in a place with lots of Dots. I set that thought aside; my more immediate problem was surviving life with this Dot for who knows how long. Wit and speed had gotten me out of trouble many times before, but I doubted that would work on a long-term basis with someone like her at this level of proximity. Somehow, I had to be useful; I had to be the prisoner who pulls the bully's strings.

It was a lot easier than I guessed. Here in Broomhell, locked away with the other young criminals, my smarts turned out to be a very useful resource.

* * *

Young criminals abounded. Another was Sally.

Sally was my age. She was our prized and rare animal at Broomhell: a real live nymphomaniac. The room almost applauded when she told us, girls cheering and thumping and kicking each other. We had loads of questions. Turned out, the definition of a nymphomaniac was Sally's father's when he caught her having sex with her boyfriend in the kitchen. Just the once, though. He labelled her a nympho, and Sally lived up to it.

'Jist the once?'

'You heard me.'

'Jeesus!'

Even then I knew better than to believe the story was that simple, but anyway, Sally seemed to embrace it and played her part. And thus, we formed our gang.

Next in age was tall, skinny, dark-haired Lorraine. Sent from foster parent to foster parent for as long as she could remember, Lorraine was a runaway. That was her 'crime'. It seemed that no one at Broomhell knew the rest of her story, and Lorraine certainly never spoke of it. She was quiet, timid, got along with everyone—even the most treacherous bitches among us—and was left pretty much alone.

'What's her fuckin' story then?' I asked Dot.

'Mind yer ane business.'

Then there was Annie; Annie was thirteen. Apparently, Annie's parents just couldn't cope with her. It was hard to understand because Annie was always fun, a bit crazy, but bright. Another tragic victim of a broken home, her open face was always pleased to see me; one could see the beautiful things of the world shining through her eyes. Her innocence won Annie immunity, even from Dot's hard shell. Annie was epileptic and the rest of us became experts in looking after her, her fits providing entertainment in an otherwise boring day.

Then there was this tiny wee toot of a thing. I swear she was only nine or thereabouts. She spent every other weekend locked up at Broomhell. Perhaps one of her sets of parents or stepparents sent her to the hostel so that they could have respite—just my guess, that's all. Small wonder some of us became criminals. This tiny tot had done nothing wrong and there she was in this crazy 'hostel' with us.

That brings me to our caretaker, Matron.

A short, ugly bull of a woman, Matron's bright red dyed hair was piled high on top, a clip comb holding together the bedraggled French roll that framed a hard face with its broken nose, thick smeared crimson lipstick, and droopy blue eyes. Years of drinking gave her the look of a perpetual hangover. A few drinks after supper would get Matron bawling. Sometimes, we'd hear the taxi driver, 'her boyfriend', skulking through the corridor, sneaking into her room late at night. I never once saw a hint of warmth from that woman for the whole four or five months that I was there. It was her and us—but of course, that made the 'us' much more.

For amusement, we played the usual pranks. Depositing a turd outside Matron's door, knocking and scarpering and giggling. One night a crowd of boys queued up in the garden, each taking their turn to shimmy up the drainpipe and jump into bed with Sally the nymph. One of the girls collected the 'entrance fee' in the garden below; another helped tug and yank the boy in through the bathroom window, then ushered him through when it was his turn. Bored, we'd run away, fleeing the gates of Broomhell.

'Hurry up, for fuck's sake!'

'Fit aboot Dot?'

''At cunt'll be a'right! Fuckin' hurry!'

We never got very far but we did get the thrill of being escorted back to our hostel in a police car with the siren screaming. It was something to do.

Unlikely as it seems, Broomhell was where I began growing up. I started having my periods there, to the chuckles of the other girls. I got my first job, a local government post, pricing prescriptions for the NHS. Our supervisor was a sweet-faced woman, who understood all girls went through a phase. I'm not sure if she felt sorry for me, reasoning I'd be dead before I turned twenty, but knowing I had her silent support somehow helped. I was able to walk to work and I enjoyed living near the centre of town. I went out every weekend, went on the pill, got fat, and got bored. I needed something to pass the time. Devilment and drama had become a necessity for my mental survival, and who better to play it out with than MICK MASSIVE.

* * *

Mick was a local hardman, replete with bushy 1970s moustache, bulbous broken nose, and an eye for the best-looking women in town. He was reputed to have fathered over thirty kids, to be the top street fighter, and to have the biggest cock in all of Aberdeen. This reputation Mick was happy to prove by whipping said appendage out and slapping it on the barroom table as the crowd guffawed and placed bets. There was one larger willy in town, but unfortunately attached to a body so un-fuckable that the tale is not worth recounting.

Such was the Saturday afternoon entertainment in the bars around Aberdeen's harbour.

At the time I was waitressing weekends at the Carlton, a pub only minutes away from the lowlife haunts of Market Street, where Mick's crowd gathered. There was a gang of them, mostly older guys out drinking, fighting, and whoring. Aberdeen's gangster world. My girlfriend Cathy gave me the lowdown: 'That's Mick Massive eyeing you up!' she whispered as we stood in our platform soles under the 'Waitresses Only' sign waiting for our trays to be filled. 'Mick's got bairns a' o'er the place. Scott's his favourite; he's got a soft spot for his ma.'

'Fit? Shut the fuck up!'

'Watch yersel', he's jist a whoormayster, an' he's gan' steady wi' Tracy Bruce, she's really bonny, ye winna tak 'im awa' fae her.' I was young, not quite sixteen, a little chubby, and Tracy was beautifully slim. I was flattered Mick was even looking, although I couldn't quite see what the attraction to this man was myself. At five foot nine he was short and stocky. His gingery moustache seemed to have a life of its own and twitched when he looked at me from under shaggy eyebrows, making his intentions quite plain. The poor man didn't even have the gift of the gab—in fact, Mick was a mumbler. I wondered if he had mumbled and twitched his women into bed? Or perhaps it was his loud unbuttoned shirts showing off his chest hair, and the pale pea-green hip-hugging trousers that left little to the imagination. *There he is, ladies and gentlemen, for all to see, the town cock!*

Mick was both a challenge and a chance to shoot myself to local 'fame'. Shameful and stupid, yes, there was also a history of self-abuse, a theme already well established within me. I didn't even consider not going there; my early refusals only sparked a keener interest, and Mick Massive wasn't one for taking no for an answer.

On the night I 'gave in', we went back to a flat after the dancing. We didn't even bother with the proffered cup of tea but made straight for the bedroom. As soon as the door closed behind us, Mick started ripping off his clothes, revealing this massively muscular, hairy chest. Fuck, this is grown-up! I looked around, making sure none of Mick's pals were spying through the window to witness this. Seeing nothing else for it, I took off my clothes. The bedroom was freezing. 'Are ye caul, quine?'

'BRRRRRRRRR.' I hunkered over the bars on the little electric fire thinking I didn't feel sexy at all. It was one of those *feel the fear and do it anyway* moments. So off we went—BUMP, BUMP, BUMP. He stretched me. I'd never had painful fucks before; I'd heard women complain of it, but this was a first for me.

'Oh God, *yeah!*' Mick screeched at the end, climbing off me, wringing wet.

Would I ever be the same again? I was shivering and drunk. I don't remember pleasure. I do remember thinking, *Well I've done it, I've just fucked Mick Massive.*

That was it. It was the beginning of … what, exactly? Something. I'm not even sure if I can call it a love affair. It was the start of Saturday nights with Mick, and he was certainly someone I wanted to master.

Saturday nights we rolled into various flats, bedsits, council houses, places Mick had earmarked for shagging purposes. One time he gave me a black eye. I hadn't expected that. People took notice; I was Mick Massive's chick and when I got chatted up at the dancing, inevitably someone would come and warn the guy off. It wouldn't be long before Tracy Bruce would find out and feel the pressure on her throne.

While the intrigue of being a small-town gangster babe was entertaining, it was not nearly as interesting as working on my master plan: the great escape.

Things were changing within me. At Broomhell, we often came into the spotlight of the authorities. We ran away often, each time the police caught us, blubbering, 'Please, please, don't take us back.' I was not slow in telling the police and my probation officer about Matron's boozing, and how wrong it was that a little nine-year-old was in the same place as borstal-bound Dot. Meanwhile, my urge to violence seemed to diminish with the onset of my periods, and things were improving with my parents. We'd survived several weekend visits home—even the one where I'd sneaked Mick out in the morning covered in make-up so I could say he was my 'girlfriend'.

At the next Children's Panel meeting we decided to put up a united front. It worked. I was clear with my parents about my ambitions to leave Aberdeen and travel. Compromise came in the shape of a job offer via the Guernsey Tourist Board. This was safe enough to convince my parents, and in April 1974, aged seventeen, off I went.

This was it. Freedom! Goodbye, rules and home!

I remember myself on the day I officially left. Tight skirt just above the knee. Loads of eyeshadow. Breasts bursting out of my clothes due to the contraceptive pills that my friends and I pumped ourselves full of. A later generation would pay that price. Even if we'd known I doubt it would have stopped us, such was the allure of avoiding unwed pregnancies.

As I packed my suitcase, I remember my dread of the cold and my fear of insomnia. Both pretty near the top of a junkie's list of fears, fears that are with me to this day. Perhaps it was some weird premonition that I felt back in 1974 whilst getting ready for the overnight bus that was going to take me from Aberdeen forever.

The antidote: a Mogadon from my grandma, a half bottle of Whisky Mac in my backpack, and wrapped up in the warmest clothes I possessed. As I huddled in the bus's back seat and waited for the wheels to start turning, my heart went out to my mother as she stood waving goodbye. I often thought about her standing there, crying her eyes out. It's one of the stories she repeated in her foggy Alzheimer days: 'I knew I had to let you go, I didn't want to, but I knew I had to. You were away to do all the things I wished I could. I didn't have the nerve, but you did.'

As I look back, I wonder how much my mum and dad knew. Did they really believe I was somehow 'wicked'? Or did they realise I'd been hurt and just couldn't find the words? They certainly knew about Mick Massive; Christ, the whole town did! That would have been realisation enough that the best thing was to take me to the station. Yet weepy goodbyes from my parents or not, off I went, counting the miles under my wheels, and me with tears streaming a river down my face.

CHAPTER THREE

Guernsey

My arrival in Guernsey was glorious. Saint Peter Port with its pretty shimmering harbour glittered before me, overlooked by climbing slopes with narrow steps and cobbled streets housing pubs that stayed open all day. The lush countryside and the sparkling white beaches cried out my name, the town's long and winding country roads easily negotiable by bike. All summer long I explored, cycled and swam, shedding both the schoolgirl weight and much of what had left me feeling imprisoned in Aberdeen. I underwent a metamorphosis, like a caterpillar crawling out of its cocoon, transforming into a butterfly.

However, my first destination—the family-run Shaggy-Ha Hotel—was neither the imaginary oasis nor the holy sanctum nor the utopia it claimed to be. Instead, it resembled an even more chaotic and dysfunctional 'Fawlty Towers' on steroids.

'Family-run' meant, in fact, only five of us: Samuel, the hapless father; Daisy, his neurotic wife; Cook, the hotel's tipsy chef; Judy, the other chambermaid/waitress; and me.

Judy was my sidekick on this adventure: raven straight hair to my blonde curls, piercing blue eyes to my soft brown ones, and Yorkshire to my Scottish. A fellow Scorpio, intense and rebellious, she had also been through enough turmoil in her short life yet continued on her doomed quest for self-improvement. Because of this, we hit it off instantly.

Cook was another matter. Eighty-four years old, she was totally mad and beautifully batshit in the most glorious of ways. A gargantuan woman, Cook was skin and bones with a dried-out tuft of strawberry-blonde hair on top. Ruby-red lipstick smashed across her lips and bright blue eyes told me, despite the outward damaged shell, that this woman had once lived, and loved. Cook was an alcoholic. She wouldn't have put up with the treatment that Swiss Family Fawlty dished out otherwise. She lived in a stinking old caravan and worked her socks off.

The deal was that Judy and I would supply Cook with pints of lager all day. We'd pull her seven pints or more and then she would go on to neat whiskey at night. Cook's liver was a well-oiled machine. The pints just kept her topped up as she cooked hot tomato soup, fish and chips, Poire belle Hélène or peach Melba.

We were the dream team. Not once did either the owner's lazy son or daughter lift a finger to help when they waddled home from whatever posh English boarding school they attended. The wife, Daisy, poor soul, did make spasmodic, albeit pathetic, efforts in between her psychotic 'breakdowns' when they would either cart her off in a straitjacket or Daisy would mysteriously disappear during the night.

Complete lunacy ruled at the Shaggy-Ha. Work started early. We'd get a bang on the door from Samuel, groan our way out of bed and stagger into our white blouses, black skirts, and tights, tying the white apron strings behind our still-aching backs as we plodded and trooped downstairs to prepare for breakfast. Two choices of fruit juice, cereal, tea or coffee, toast, butter, and jams delivered with a tip-provoking smile while taking the orders for Cook. Serving up, clearing up, washing up, setting up for dinner. Making every single bed in the house. Some general housework and then, the blessed break.

'Oy, Vic, no rest for the wicked!'

'Tell me about it!'

The pace was hectic—maddening. Slumped from exhaustion, I revelled in those precious stolen hours consumed in my personal mission of making the absolute most of my time in Guernsey. These were hours I spent alone, methodically exploring beach after beach courtesy of the pushbike I borrowed (some might say *thieved*) from the hotel. Some of the beaches were deserted enough that I could peel off my clothes and run stark naked into the crashing surf, leaping into the frothy white waves, laughing at the universe's twists and turns. Life was grand! I felt so free! Content, I'd scurry back to work in time to serve supper. By the time the washing up was finished and with the limited bus service, trips to town had to be planned or taken on our evening off at the weekend. So mostly our evenings were spent imprisoned in our dreary rooms in the hotel.

At the beginning of the season, with the kids still away at school and the hotel relatively quiet, Judy and I had a room on the lower floor, with two single beds, a dressing table and a window looking out to the back garden; it reminded me of the window at primary school where I'd often sit gazing, time standing still, lost in thought. Some evenings we would sit on our beds, girl-talking and gossiping and swapping stories of loves lost and won; some we'd write home with our news of Guernsey, reading out letters received, making plans for shopping trips and a night on the town. As the hotel got busier, we would get shunted from room to room, some as dumpy and cramped as a broom closet. 'Isn't *this* fuckin' woeful?' 'Jeesus, that's a great smell comin' from the bathroom.' This resulted in one bizarre night while Daisy was 'away' and Samuel offered us the best room in the house.

We thought nothing of it; the room was empty, so his evil ploy didn't cross our minds. Giggling like schoolgirls, we were bouncing on the bed in our nighties when the swarthy, sly bastard came in and jumped in beside us. Surprised, but not slow, neither of us cowered at the five-foot-two Jew, and like a professional tag team, we shoved him off the bed booting him firmly out of the door, which we hastened to lock. Then we both fell back on the bed, cracking up with laughter.

Next day was a different story. I was incensed. That cunning swine! Swiss Family Fawlty had gotten my working-class dander up. To be fair, despite being a slut-chasing sleazebag, Samuel was a grafter; it was the other three family members who were a pitiful mixture of pathetic and institutionalised entitlement. Perhaps Samuel, the third Scorpio in the house, felt entitled sexually, but that was not happening on Judy's and my watch.

'What do we do?'

'Wha' d'ye mean?'

'Samuel! He's our fuckin' boss!'

'Any messin' and I'll kill 'im, that's wha'!'

The more I thought about it, the angrier I got. How dare the old geezer even think about it! After several days brooding on it, I came up with the perfect sting. I painstakingly typed out two documents on the hotel's heavy old silver typewriter: a letter addressed to the Guernsey Tourist Board, and a new contract promising us girls a double bonus at the end of the season. Horror-struck, Samuel realised right away he had no option but to sign and he deserved to be pulled up—and we deserved that bonus.

Surprisingly, the season went well after that. Samuel only sulked for a short while. As the Shaggy-Ha got busier, Judy and I simply learnt new tricks and moved faster. Soon one of us was preparing the sweets ahead of time while the other took the orders. Cook even let us have a go at frying up breakfast, chummying up enough to share her secret culinary tips. Over several watered-down whiskeys and a quiet night in the bar she'd let slip to us girls some of her youth back in 1930s Ireland. Tales of lost loves and a life in service. Other nights, I enjoyed chatting to the guests who booked the hotel on holiday. Judy didn't often join us; she'd lock herself in her room working out the hurt that had brought her here. Through the door I'd hear her burst into tears. Oh God, why is life so painful? I could see Judy was consumed by sadness, although I believe my own joie de vivre and willingness to move on and grow helped her enormously. It was just that schmoozing and hobnobbing with the guests was a step too far for Judy.

My problem: I was only seventeen. Still too young to see that happiness would not come from love, wealth, or sex. Utterly bored and unsatisfied just sitting in my room waiting for work in the morning, I begged and pleaded with Samuel to show me the ropes behind the bar. Unlocking my inner bitch forced him to give in.

The Shaggy-Ha bar became my sanctuary. It wasn't huge but the decor was tasteful: a beautifully polished wooden counter overlooked upholstered benches. Cook often sat opposite the bar, diminutive as a troll as she thrust her whiskey to grateful lips. With Daisy only rarely popping in, and Judy in her room, it was during those evenings that we three built up a rapport. Samuel, white half coat cast aside in favour of slacks and shirt; me, now a sun-kissed blonde in my best barmaid frock; Cook, bony old hand knocking back drink after drink then scurrying out with the double Samuel always poured her as the guests trickled in. I felt very grown-up; this was the first time I'd held conversations with adults other than parents, teachers and social workers. Not only that, but these adults seemed genuinely interested in what I had to say, often making comments on my adventurousness, and daring.

They saw things in me that I hadn't—not yet. Cliché or not, I had spontaneously combusted from the wasteland of Aberdeen and emerged phoenix-like. And I was starting to see myself in a new light.

* * *

As the weather grew warmer and the Shaggy-Ha became squeezed with guests, Judy and I were moved into the chalet at the bottom of the garden. Apart from the bitter chill at night and having to walk over the lawn getting grass all over our shoes, we liked it.

One day, Daisy—'Mrs S' as we called her—strolled over to visit. Her summer dress with sparkling green and blue flowers spattered over a white background moved from the waist down in a way I only now recognise is reserved for the most expensive of cuts. I didn't need to know that; I hated her anyway. Mrs S had a way of gazing at you through watery blue-green eyes that made you realise in one second flat that she would rather drop dead than give you the time of day. Those vacant eyes may well have had the life sucked from them by the loathsome vampire husband who slithered through that house. Although Judy and I got on well with Samuel now, I had seen the other side of him, the evil intent that flashed through the slits of his ebony eyes. Daisy's evil intent was slimier, more secretive, yet even she tried to use us.

It wasn't long before the opportunity arose to call her out.

It was around this time that Cathy's brother Trevor, and their cousin Jerry—with his black piratey beard and sparkling Irish eyes—landed in Guernsey. The dynamic duo hadn't managed to secure accommodation within their budget of no doubt next to nothing when I received a phone call SOS from Cathy.

'Will ye help?'

'Only because I hate the fuckin' sight of ye.'

'Fuck yourself, that's lovely.'

Unwilling to leave family stranded, Judy and I agreed we would double up with them in the chalet. There was a back lane with a private gate to the garden, so it was feasible our secret guests would remain hidden, at least for the short term.

Soon Cathy's family arrived; and destiny revealed its sinister hand.

Around this same time, the situation with Daisy was coming to a head. A superficial relationship with her husband, clear disrespect from her children, unable—or perhaps not allowed—to join us in the bar, Daisy didn't know what to do with her evenings. Thus, it was this fateful night she invited Judy and me to join her at the Ouija board.

Intrigued, we duly turned up at the appointed hour. Ouija was quite the rage at the time; we'd heard horror stories of teenagers with homemade boards using it as a tool of the devil, communicating with spirits and raising the dead. We presumed these were scare tactics, yet as we marched into the dining room to discover Daisy sitting at a circular table, her face lit by flickering candles and melodrama, things started to look bleak. After telling us the rules and gripping our hands, the spooky seance began. The Ouija pointer started careening and flying across the board. The walls rattled and my chest started thumping. I was familiar with the feeling of the unfamiliar, but this was unexpected; moments later, my paternal grandfather came through with messages no one else could have known.

'Judy?'

'Yeah?'

'Did ye hear that?'

'I'm goin' to be sick!'

Judy slapped a hand over her mouth, to keep from puking. The suspense in the room was palpable. I felt shaken. There was something very disturbing about opening that energy with someone like Daisy in the room. I resolved to leave. Unfortunately, that was easier said than done.

Daisy became more and more demanding, claiming the Ouija only worked when I was there. 'You're fuckin' crazy!' I screamed. Finally, I'd had enough. Snatching her arm, I dragged her to one side: 'Mrs S, it only works like that for me because I am a member of a coven!' I blurted out.

Daisy thought about it. She was fascinated. 'What do I have to do to join?'

I let my face give that answer. 'Our chief warlock is coming to visit soon,' I said, thinking of Cathy's cousin Jerry. My inner bitch knew no bounds.

Jerry, however, was harder to convince: 'There's no way I'm shagging that old bird!' he squawked.

'You don't have to shag anybody,' I pleaded. 'Just lie on the bed looking mysterious and see how far she goes.' Unfortunately, that wasn't doing it. Jerry refused. Fortunately, I had an accomplice. Trevor, who had always been on the podgy, can't-be-bothered side and happy to lie lazily all day in the chalet keeping out of sight, had always been good for a prank, especially if he was only the voyeur. Anyway, Trevor undoubtedly would be grateful for any offering of a shag. This did the trick, and the scene was set.

In charge of wardrobe, I garbed Jerry in his best white shirt, unbuttoned to the waist, revealing furry black chest hair adorned with one of Judy's hippy necklaces. I shoved one of his socks down his skin-tight flares to emphasise nature's offering and showed him how to lie provocatively on the bed as Daisy opened the door. The deal was this: Trevor would watch from behind the kitchenette partition and come to the rescue if required. I would have done anything to be the director on the set, or even a fly on the wall to see Daisy's face. However, the best Judy and I could allow ourselves was a vantage point from the bedroom window. There we stood, eyes peeking over the sill, hands between our crossed legs to stop from wetting ourselves, as dear Daisy minced her way to the chalet. Job done!

Soon it was time for the boys to move on from the Shaggy-Ha. They found cheap digs in town, allowing us to enjoy their company in Guernsey a little longer. I took Jerry on my skinny-dipping tour while Trevor lazed around drinking daytime pints. The four of us even managed to squeeze in a pub crawl. Life was good.

Already aware of my inner growth, it wasn't long before I realised the same was happening on the outside. On the odd occasion Judy and I made it to town, I noticed that the level of attention I attracted was becoming a distraction. As we passed, perverted heads bent, and eyes stared freely at my breasts. Judy wasn't impressed. 'How have ye managed this now? Ye look fuckin' useless to me.' It wasn't only the young men either. On those afternoons where I had opted for sitting in the garden reading a romantic novel or writing my juiciest adventures in my diary, I would sometimes have a cuppa with Old Tom next door. I loved sitting in his greenhouse or strolling down the rows and rows of tomatoes listening to all Tom knew about growing them. I had seen the old fellow sneakily checking me out, though he tried to hide it.

One day Tom told me I should be a model. At first, I took it as flirty flattery, yet Tom refused to let it go. He was determined to get the penny to drop.

'But Tom! I'm not nearly tall enough!' I scoffed.

'It doesn't matter, you could be a photographic model, you'd look great in pictures,' Old Tom said, drooling. And so it went on. Eventually he persuaded me to enter the Miss Guernsey beauty contest—something I have never quite forgiven him for, since I only came in third! Never mind! Mum—who had come to visit with my two younger sisters—was delighted, and to give Tom his due, the old bugger had planted more than a tomato seed.

Yet, oh God, I was so depressed! At the end of the season—with the collection of jewellery I'd bought myself from the £12 a week we earned but rarely spent, and a decent double bonus—I boarded a ferry, so glad to leave Guernsey, yet enriched by my experience. Initially

I was happy to go home, with my reports of how it was in the big world outside our Doric doors. My friends loved to hear me describe the discotheque and day-long drinking that made nightlife in Guernsey far exceed anything on offer in Aberdeen. The same was true of the young men: 'They're a' poofs, ye cin get them ti buy ye drinks a' night, 'n the dinna even ask ye for a snog!' I told it that way to appear unchanged, to fit in—but the words soured on my tongue. My trip away had made me realise that was not the true story: in the big world there were both cultural and social differences that I had never considered before.

I passed the dreich, dark Aberdonian winter with temping work at the new BP building out of the city, a position made possible by the growing oil and gas industry, my minimal qualifications, and the gift of the gab. The man who owned the temp agency knew my father and told him later, 'You won't ever need to worry about her,' as they both laughed at my gall in asking for more money during my first job interview. Things stepped up with Mick—but flattered as I was at dethroning his previous lover (or so Mick told me), Market Street pubs and small-town gangsters had lost their appeal. I was stagnating. It was June before I wised up to it, and the tomato-picking jobs I had intended applying for in Jersey would be gone by now.

Nevertheless, wanderlust had got me, the road called my name, and desperate measures were called for. I persuaded my friend Kiki to come with me, and with only £17 between us, we stood with our tiny rucksacks on the Stonehaven Road with our thumbs out, ready to hitch south, showers of spiky sunlight in our eyes, hoping to leave the likes of Aberdeen forever.

CHAPTER FOUR

Jersey

I had learnt a lot in the four years since I first hit the road. I possessed enough worldliness to survive and enough game to take what I wanted, and those few pounds we left home with not only got us to Jersey but kept us going for a month.

To supplement our trip, Kiki and I posed in doorways as young hookers, skirts halfway up our thighs asking for 'cash up front', then legged it on the way to 'the room'. There was also sweet old Stan—who was more than satisfied with our sticky, under-the-table hand-holding in the restaurant, in return for which he bought us a fair share of steak suppers. At the same time, I had a fling with a smouldering Italian waiter, which gave us a bed any night we fancied and a top-notch staff breakfast in the morning.

'Fuck off,' Kiki always moaned in envy, 'I'm nae fighting off 'at greaser a' night while you're rumpy pumpin' lover boy: "Oh, Tony Macaroni, gees yer I-ty sassidge!"'

'Fuck off, *you,*' I snapped back. 'I niver said 'at, he's nae that good onywy, ooo, bella, bella, bellahhhhhh!' I dry-humped her leg in exaggerated ecstasy, laughing.

'Fuck sake, a'right then!'

Oh God, were we flirtatious! There were plenty of parks and beaches and heaps of public toilets for dressing up and putting on gobs of make-up. Darling, I still have the snapshots to prove it! However, it was only that, a joy ride, my heart wasn't in it; despite having become quite the expert, hustling and bumming weren't for me. I was paying lip service to a dream I had now outgrown. And I wasn't really bothered about tomato picking or the 'even better' discos and clubs than Guernsey. My sights were now set elsewhere, and it wasn't long in coming.

Realising Jersey is not that big a place, I started to feel things might go wrong if we carried on. Thus, despite Kiki's protests, I put our last few coins in the slot and telephoned Mum and Dad. 'We canna hear ye, quine, far are ye? Fit ye deein'? Ye need money for *fit?* Fa the bloody hell is Kiki?' Kiki was a year younger, and just as she feared, ended up getting shipped back to Aberdeen to face the music. Me, I boarded my first ever flight, destination: London.

Landing there, and owing my mum £11 for the flight, it was time to get a job. I went straight to Mick's mum and dad's in Harlesden; fuck me, I hated it, but it would have to do. I had no intention of being sent home weeping on the bus ever again.

You might ask why I returned to Mick. I've asked myself that question many times. Like a season in the sun, that little Mick dream was no longer one that took up the airtime in my head—true in many ways it was a backward step, but the answer was easy. I was only a kid when I started to dream of going to London and working in a boutique on the King's Road or Carnaby Street. I watched my older cousins in their teeny tight miniskirts, beehive hairdos and glittery hoop earrings, and wanted to be at the heart of all that. In my early teens I listened to tales of 'famous' Aberdonians—as if there were some—who now 'had their own flat in London'.

These were the teen dreams of young Vicki, dreams that sustained me through unhappy years. I had always felt misplaced, misguided, remembered being constantly bored, schoolwork was no challenge, I didn't have friends, no sisters or brothers. I do have some fond memories of the boy next door, Georgie Porgy, and his electric train set, but he moved away when we were very young. The others in the tenement were horrible to me. Putting a posh school uniform on me was akin to painting a bullseye on my back. I regularly climbed the stairs in tears with a bloody nose, bruised knees, even a head once split wide open by a spade. That continued until my father, sick of seeing his little girl bullied, showed me how to wield the big stick he'd cut for me on a day trip to the countryside. That put an end to the beatings, but not to my loneliness. I was rejected by the girlfriends my mother, trying to slake her own ambitions, shoved me towards at school, and was ten before I made my first bestie, a shy young lass named Claire.

Claire came from a huge family. Their clothes were cast-offs and hand-me-downs, something my mother's working-class pride would never allow. The parents were teachers; the children's ambitions were intellectual and creative. They had a wooden hut out in the countryside, not far from where I live now, with massive built-in double bunks where Claire and I would gossip and chat long past midnight. The never-ending days were spent strolling through marshes watching baby birds hatch, climbing hillsides, and sitting in trees. Magically Claire knew what animal would stroll by next, having spent her whole childhood summers there. 'Ye didn't turn up on Tuesday, Mr Otter, far hiv ye been? Gettin' big, Mrs Hedgehog, fit a size yer belly is, is 'at nae sair? And how are ye, little pheasant? Yer looking chipper!' Her mystical, otherworldly ways stunned me. My time with her was a reprieve from what was fast becoming an unbearable fluctuating post-pubescent mess between frozen awkwardness and mad lashing out at the world.

At home, staring out my bedroom window, beyond the swing park, the other council houses sloping down towards the bleak grey city, everything screamed of escape. I just wanted to leave, to get away and never come back. The first time I ran away was to Edinburgh. I was in first year and I found myself standing in the school office numbing up for the inevitable telling-off, when I spotted them: a huge roll of green dinner tickets with black print and perforated joins staring up at me. They were even the colour of money. The sixth former prefect, deep in her own story, undoubtedly a fantasy of the praise about to be bestowed upon her for reporting me for whatever indiscretion that had caused her to drag me up there in the first place, wouldn't have considered how swiftly I might have stuffed anything of value into my school bag. Just too fucking easy. I couldn't wait to tell Jana.

Jana, the fuckin' slut that she was, was a latecomer to the high school. Who knows how she ended up at such a posh institution—the way she told it, her story began and ended with the fact she was a Gypsy. Yes, like the Cher song—she certainly looked like a young Cher with her dark, gold-speckled green eyes and tight tawny skin. The spoiling of what would have been a wild beauty was this one canine tooth in Jana's massive jutting jaw, which gave her a satanic appearance. I wouldn't have been surprised to catch her sticking pointy pins in dolls and practising voodoo if she thought no one was around. Certainly, later, after she got her sharp claws into my boyfriend, she snottily explained: 'I just asked him if he wanted to see my tan and when I showed him my belly …'

As if animal lust was mitigation for breaking a girl's rule—with my own fuckin' boyfriend, like! Anyway, that came later—that day, as if I'd won the lottery, I gleefully held up the dinner tickets. 'Look what I've got! We're selling them!' And we did, loads of them. Later when the summons came, we knew someone had snitched. I pleaded with Jana: 'Let's go before they get us,' and we slipped out the back gate next to the bicycle shed, sneaky striding legs tiptoeing all the way down the back lane that separated the tall town houses from the mansions on Albyn Place. 'Come on, stupid, now *run!*' I hollered, bold as brass. Out of school bounds we openly scooted down the backstreets to Aberdeen joint station then hopped on a train. *Phew!* It was possible to do that back in those days; no barriers, no turnstiles, no security guards looking for runaways and fraudsters. Big Brother was yet to awake! We simply leapt on board then hid out in the toilet the whole journey. During those three bumpy hours we shed our school shirts and ties, stuffed the ties in our school bags, wore the shirts back to front so the front looked like white polo necks, hitched our skirts up and turned our school blazers inside out. 'London, here we come!' In my head, that's where we were running off to, though neither of us had thought to check the sign at the front of the train. It turned out the train only went as far as Edinburgh. For fuck's sake! As if we'd escaped house arrest, we roamed wildly around the city a while—that is, until the sun set and it started to get dark, then we got scared. We reported ourselves to a policeman who dragged us to the police station and phoned my dad.

'She did *fit*'? Jesus bloody Christ, fit next, the little bugger, wait till I get my hands on her. Christ fits 'er ma gan ti dee wi 'er. No, no, al come for 'er! Fit's the address? Am on my wy!'

Dad confessed to me later how with hardly any petrol in the car, freewheeling as much of the way as he could, he drove down to Edinburgh to fetch us. A farmer topped up our tank on the way home. I only discovered that piece during the last year of Dad's life. A time when I shared as much of my shocking story as I could with him and indeed, he his, parts of his life that I had never known before. It was only in that telling that I saw love in his words and actions. Back then, I only saw a jailer come to take me back into custody and lock me away.

That was the first time I tried to run away from home. After that, my goal was more clearly defined: London. And I got there several times, but I never lasted more than a night.

Yet I refused to quit. More determined than ever, I continued to plot my escape from home. Finally, I arrived in London with not much more than an Underground ticket in my pocket, and no forwarding address at which to stay. Mick's mum and dad lived there, so it was simple: I went to live with them.

Mick's parents, Johnny, and Elsie, puzzled me. Johnny moved to Aberdeen after the shipbuilding on the Clyde declined, where he settled with his wife and their four kids until he upped sticks and left for London with his new mistress, Elsie. To say 'Elsie' and 'mistress' in the same sentence still throws me to this day. Elsie was a guarded islander, a frigid cow, who looked more like Queen Victoria than a temptress. She wore blouses buttoned to her neck, and dressing gowns double-wrapped and double-belted. 'Mistress? Elsie?' my young mind pondered, how did that happen? Both she and Mick's dad worked packing baked beans at the big factory in Wembley. They rented the ground floor of a rambling Victorian house, home to hundreds of mice. All I knew of mice was Mum's stories of Grandma clobbering them with her rolling pin as they scuttled around the pantry.

Mick himself found work on a building site, and I registered with a temping agency. We slept in bunk beds in the cramped spare room. It felt temporary and unwelcoming. I lived out of my backpack with the next day's outfit hanging from the top bunk. Every night Elsie would 'cook' horrible gluey things in tin cans from the shop at work while the men guzzled down beer. I'd pop into the kitchen from time to time offering a hand. It was never accepted. She'd look down her nose, the notion clearly horrifying; she never said it out loud, but her face showed she thought I was fuckin' useless and wanted me out from under her feet. 'Just you leave me to get on with it!' the uptight bitch lied. My talents were reserved for washing the dishes. Sometimes Elsie went to bingo and Johnny went to bed early with more beer. Mick and I watched TV or when she was out, we fucked.

This was my 'Heinz Beanz existence', and I was bored out of my skull.

Even the hoped-for blissful Saturday night out—which I thought would be a trip into the West End—meant downtown boring Harlesden and cheap drinks at Johnny's work's social club. Much as I hated it, I satisfied myself knowing I was just a small step away from the real London. Meanwhile I looked for an excuse to walk out on Mick. Did I feel a twinge of guilt? Perhaps. I occupied myself earning money, buying new clothes, and going about everyday life. It was only when I felt a craving to explore that I twigged on that I was virtually a prisoner there.

'Can wi nae go for a walk?'

'Fuck 'at for a cayray on! Place is full o' muggers.'

'Fit aboot 'at new pub?'

'They're ay queuein' doon i street. We'll niver get in.'

'I heard there's duncin' at i jazz club.'

''At shite, it's too loud ony-y.'

'The West End then?'

'Too fuckin' dear. Fuck's sake, are ye niver pleased?'

We literally did nothing else but eat from cans, drink from cans, fuck, or watch TV. Worse, I couldn't even enjoy their TV programmes, which they piped at extreme volume. One night they were too roaring drunk to notice so I managed to sneak out to the phone box tucked behind the railway bridge and call my girlfriend Cathy.

'Fit's adee, ye fed up wi' his big tager a'ready?'

'Och, it's nae that, I'm bored outta ma *miiiind*, fuckin' beans ivry night, am nae even allowed doon here ti the phone box!'

'He'll be feert ye rin awa' wi' a darky wi' an even bigger 'een!' Cathy cackled, yet she knew I needed out and we spent the rest of the call plotting and scheming my getaway.

I lay awake a few more nights rehearsing the plan. *Save up my money. Masses of money. Chuck it away. Must get eyebrows plucked. Legs shaved before the trip. No more malingering.* On the first day that I was last to leave in the morning, I packed my bag and jumped on the train to a boarding house I'd found in the paper in Battersea.

Battersea had a different feel altogether from Harlesden, although still not quite right for me. Apart from anything else, the £30 a night room seemed extortionate, but it was clean and had good locks on the door. Fuck me, I wasn't planning to stay long anyway. I'd walk down to the nearest cafe picking up the *London Weekly Advertiser* on the way and search the Situations Vacant columns over a fry-up with lots of strong tea. There I found the answer to my prayers: '*Glamour Models Wanted!*' It pulsated out of the page at me as if in neon. The drum roll beat—yes, it's true, opportunities galore, this is it! I quite fancied my chances of being a model—my older cousin Irene used to make me up with bouffant hair, black eyeliner, and green eyeshadow so I looked like a Hollywood star, and I did, even at twelve. I knew from the countless hours I spent posing in the mirror that I could pull it off. The make-up gave me a facade that I loved to play with, and like Narcissus I marvelled at and fell in love with my own reflection.

But a glamour model? Me? Tom the tomato man and the horny photographer from Aberdeen's *The Press and Journal* had both portrayed me as an 'up-and-coming' glamour girl. I reckoned I had what it took and now I was getting my chance. In my eighteen-year-old brain I imagined the starry sight of my future: 'Oh, I'll be posing in lingerie adverts and stuff like that, maybe an underwear catalogue!' Delighted by my fantasy, I snatched some change and a pen and went to the phone box to find out more.

'Yeah,' sniffed the girl who answered the phone, 'it's like lingerie 'n a little bit a nude.' Conscious of my short-arse status, I asked her how tall one needed to be.

'Height's not important for glamour work.' *Brilliant,* I thought, and made the arrangements to meet her.

After hanging up, it hit me: *Fuck, if you've nae gotta be tall, maybe you've got to have big tits!* In a blur I rang her back, my hand trembling to grip the phone.

'How big does your bust have to be?'

'What size are yer boobs, luv? 34B, oh that's fine, yeah yeah yeah, no problem at all, get yourself over here, we'll have a look, yeah? Okay, see you soon, look for number twenty, ta-ra!' *Click!*

I hung up, unable to breathe. Before I knew it, I was walking out of the subway on to Piccadilly Circus; the bright lights, the massive Coca-Cola sign, colourful clothes hanging in and out of the shops, music blasting. So many people bustling and busying around, tourists of every shape, size and colour. I was mesmerised and in love—there was something about it that resonated with every part of me. My mind turned to David Copperfield with his streets paved with gold and wondered what they would have in store for me.

Turning left off Piccadilly into Wardour Street, searching the numbers for twenty, many were hidden, and it took several attempts including asking blank-faced passers-by before I homed in on the building. It housed a sex shop at ground floor level, a porn cinema in the basement and there up on the first floor I spied my Utopia: 'Miss Candy's of Wardour Street, Come Up and Photograph Us!' the words pasted on the pebbled glass window alongside silhouettes of nude women.

I was relieved to discover I could go straight up the steep stairs without having to enter the sex shop. The receptionist was not some pox-ridden tarty old hooker, as expected, but Angie from Essex. I took to her instantly and we chatted a while over a steaming cup of tea before Angie took me up the next flight of stairs to the studio.

Once inside she asked me to pop on a negligee and do a couple of poses. Trembling, I posed and preened about, looking traumatised. Angie was every bit as uncomfortable as me and quickly affirmed: 'Yeah, you'll do great.' She explained the deal: 'So right, he gets eight Polaroids 'n half an hour for a fiver, which stays with Miss Candy. Whatever you get off 'im in tips is yours, d'ya get that?' Dizzily, I nodded. 'He'll take his pick of three or four girls on that shift, so dress up to make sure you get plenty o' business, d'ya know what 'am saying?'

The studio was a long, narrow room, with a wardrobe at one end displaying all sorts of kinky clothes—spicy negligees, naughty undies, leather outfits, miniskirts, schoolgirl uniforms, you name it, they had it. Above the wardrobe there were two cupboards; one housed a camera, its lens peering through the doorknob. Angie assured me that she would be watching all the time, flipping between the two studios. 'If any o' the gents ever comes anywhere near you, I'll press the panic button under my desk … there's one here, too, luv'—pointing at the one on the wall—'and one of the guys from the shop will be up 'fore you know it and sort him out, don't you worry.' I was satisfied; in fact, it was better than I imagined.

The other end of the studio was where the action happened. The girls posed on a brown velour chair, ashtray on one side and a rubber plant on the other. Angie explained: 'Right then, luv, best to start in something sexy but not showing too much, d'ya know what I mean? Let's say a negligee with sexy undies underneath. Start with classic glamour poses asking the guy if he likes it—'How'm I doin', sir? Showin' enough leg for you?'—you know that kind of talk. They will normally ask you to see a bit more, a bit pervy like that, they might even ask you to dress up, you know something a bit weird—like in a dog collar perhaps—but that's your chance to earn tips you know! Think about it, don't go overboard but you know…you kind of get the gist of it, right, luv?' I did. Still, I wondered just how far we were expected to go. Angie must have read my mind. Girlfriend of one of the three owners, she was very clear: 'Another thing, right, this ain't a brothel; the boys would get into so much trouble for that 'cos it's illegal. You're not working girls here, right; you're just here to serve the punters. You're dressed up in the way that they want you to be dressed up. Show 'em a bit o' yer tits, bit o' yer arse 'n all that, d'ye know what I mean?' she asked, gazing at me expectantly. ''N 'at's it, y'know, *tease* 'em, *enjoy* yerselves but don't ever *touch* 'em, and they're not to touch you. But don't worry, I'm watching 'em all the time and if any of 'em step over the mark we'll be on to 'em; they're not gonna to get anywhere near you, so just wanted to make that really clear.' Good, but *working girls?* That was new to me, that was a good way of putting it.

I started working the next day, on the early shift, twelve to eight. At first, I was apprehensive—yet once I met the tough-but-charming East End guys from the shop, I was fine. What scared me was the stuff rattling inside my head: *Were my tits big enough? My belly not too fat? My legs too short? How could they want to see the inside of a fanny?* I realise now that any young lass of my era would think along those lines. I was only eighteen and not confident, just off the banana boat really. I was shy in ways that were not obvious, and it took time for me to become as bold as I eventually did. Not once did it cross my mind to question myself for being foolish, not once did I feel I was embarking on a folly. I was excited and delighted I had been chosen and about to get the education of my life.

And so, my new career in modelling began. I kept the punters at arm's length, especially the more lecherous ones, building up to do more and more. If the guy himself was shy, I'd get bold and maybe ask: 'Would you like to see my bust? I can do that for a tip. Oh, nipples as well? That's five pounds extra. Touch my own nipples? That's ten pounds.' I learnt to work out how much money the guy had. 'Oh, touch myself *down there?* Oh! that kind of shot? I'm not sure …' Until I got right up the menu to open-leg shots.

Open-leg shots were how a girl turned her body into a cash machine.

While engaging in open-leg shots, wild thoughts ranged through my head. No denying that. Some of the gents used to like, once they eyed my legs spread wide, to sniff. When I first realised that this situation was turning me on, I was shocked. *Stop obsessing, shut up, you're making good money, Vic!* I'd never been aware of being horny outside of being with a boyfriend until then, but now I noticed that showing my body in this way got *me* excited. I imagine that turned the punter on even more. There was no need to crotch-gaze to see if they had a hard-on; it was a look on their face, a gleam in their eyes, a change in their breathing. Some of them were obvious, shaking and dripping with sweat. Other times the signs were subtler. Over time, I developed this sixth sense and knew exactly the moment to say (in my best innocent schoolgirl voice): 'Would you like an open-leg shot, sir?' and there it was, £20 popped into my strategically placed handbag next to the rubber plant!

Now business was booming. Soon I had piles of cash. I hadn't known about engorged vaginas and pheromones, but I soon found out that the more I became turned on, the more fascinated the men became. Entranced by soft big brown eyes, pouting lips, soft blonde curly hair, I whispered in that young, innocent voice—'Would you like me to open my legs, sir? Would you like to see my pussy?'

Sometimes they mumbled in shock to themselves: 'Oh God … ohhh God …' Other times they had conversations with my pussy: 'Cooo! You're so beautiful!'

'Thank you,' I'd trill, 'would you like me to put my finger inside? Shall I turn round and bend over?'

That was always time for over and out.

I loved it, although much of it was unbelievable to me. I thought these men were crazy, and yet I could take as much as £200 from a punter and the most they were ever allowed to do was toss themselves off—'Have a J Arthur.' I'd discretely pass them a fistful of tissues—'Here, sir'—most of us girls didn't want to look at what the guy was doing. If they wanted us to look, then of course, that was extra. 'Five pounds for me to have a look, sir.'

The feeling of power was extraordinary, and a massive aphrodisiac. It was all in my control. They never got to touch; I couldn't have coped with them touching me, but I could—and did—get real filthy sitting in the chair miles away from them. It turned me on to do that. The East End gangsters downstairs would annihilate any guy who came near any one of us girls, so we were safe. All the punter was there for was to cough up, toss off and go slinking back into the street.

My life changed forever. It was 1976. I thought I was doing well with the London temping agencies at £44 a week, but this—fucking *amazing* this was. I felt like a queen, like the young footballers who suddenly go from nothing to making shitloads of money. I wasn't stupid with mine; money gave me security. Only five years later I bought my first flat.

* * *

Miss Candy's wasn't quite the end of my story with Mick.

Mick was waiting for me when I went to pick up my wages at the temping agency. After deep and brutally honest chit-chats, he promised we'd get our own place. And then Mick proposed. It was a bit of a dying man's last gasp, but we moved to a room in Willesden Green and enjoyed being a couple for a while. Emboldened by my new power, we did share a lot of laughs. Mick used to make me take off my knickers when I left work. He insisted on picking me up, and we'd go on the Tube separately, Mick getting turned on as he watched me flash to some guy coming home from work. It was the best of our time together, but Mick Massive was not for me.

And so as I have done so many times in my life, I made that call to Mum and Dad.

'We canna hear ye, quine, far are ye? Fit ye deein'? Mick bloody Massive! Ye better get yersel' up 'at road.'

Afterwards I told Mick I didn't really want to get married. Amazingly, he accepted, and we all went up to Aberdeen on our supposed wedding day and in good Scottish tradition, got bleezin'. During that trip I persuaded Cathy to come back with me after Christmas and I left Mick forever.

Or so I thought …

A few weeks into the new year, Cathy and I were sitting on our respective beds with their golden sheen bedspreads, sipping a late-night cuppa and making plans for flat hunting. A sudden *rap-rap-rapping* at our first-floor window silenced us mid-sentence: 'Fuckin' *burglars!*' we shrieked. Cathy jumped to her feet and armed herself with the frying pan, muttering, 'Fucking, dirty robbing bastards!' while I gawped around then picked up the sweeping brush. Fleetly she pulled back the curtains, pulled up the sash window and screamed: 'Mick fuckin' Massive! Fuck off, she's finished wi' ye, ya creep!' Mick must have shimmied up the drainpipe, the horny prick—but no sooner did his fingers gain a grip on the window ledge than Cathy deftly walloped them off. I did hear the sound—*whack!*—the fall—*thump!*—the curse—'Ooocha fucker!'—and the rustle of leaves as he hauled himself up, still hot to trot. Both Cathy and I were standing, legs crossed, absolutely pissing ourselves laughing. 'Now fuck off before we call the bobbies!' Cathy pulled the window down, wiped her hands, put them on her hips: 'Cheeky fuckin' bastard, fa dis he think he is!'

Mick hung about the streets until nearly midnight. Then the wanker moved on, hammering on doors and screaming. You could hear his voice wailing all over town. Cathy and I crawled into bed, but I didn't sleep. I just sat by the window, head draped across the sill, looking out.

CHAPTER FIVE

The Dirty Raincoat Brigade

The next time I experienced that wicked buzz as I rambled out of Piccadilly Circus station, I didn't just embrace it.

I owned it.

London. Modelling. Money. Freedom! The contrast to the cold, grey, seagull call, stinking sharp sea air, can-see-it-all place that I had come to loathe left me ecstatic. At last, I could focus on the future, and look forward to the endless possibilities of my new home!

Willesden Green was left behind with the memories of the granite city, and Cathy and I settled in West Hampstead. We soon made friends with our Irish neighbours, two sisters, Geraldine and Antoinette, and their husbands, Mick and Larry.

The rambling Victorian house—despite the dimly checked black and brown curtains that were so full of holes they had to be hooked back on nails we hammered into the wall to discourage peeping toms, and the grubby shared bathroom we nevertheless luxuriated in once a week—was home sweet home to endless fun and pranks hitherto unseen on West End Lane. The remainder of our housemates included 'the boys' from RADA; the ex-mercenary, Barry; a grey-haired lady who was rarely seen out of her dressing gown but always pleasant on the odd occasion you did meet her on the stairs; and 'Peter, Peter, shilling in the meter'.

Apart from the Irish sisters, Peter was the lodger we saw the most of. Peter stood well over six foot yet resided at the very top of the house in the sloping attic room, where he had to either stoop like Quasimodo or sit hunched on his single bed. I always wondered why he stuck with that room; I guessed he had the cheapest rent. At first glance Peter appeared rather refined, owning a full set of whiskers that were always beautifully groomed, and subtle grey flecks in his combed-back dark hair. One could easily take him for a gentleman academic or an aristocrat who had fallen out of family favour—that was, until you scanned the whole length of him. Peter's trousers never reached his ankles and always stopped a clear four inches from the ground.

Cathy noticed it first: 'Fit's adee wi' ye min', yer cat dee'd?' Peter's plum-in-the-mouth accent had no ear for our thick Scottish brogue; he always gazed blankly at these words, giving Cathy licence to repeat them over and over until she became bored of cackling at poor Peter's misfortune, hand jammed between her flannelette nightie, quilted dressing gown and legs to stop from peeing herself at her own mischievous joke.

Peter worked as a trucker. He boomed scratchy classical music on a turntable in his tiny room and earned his nickname from constantly 'chappin' at the door 'n askin' for a shillin' for the meter'. His upper-class scrounging particularly annoyed us; his posh voice had taken us in for so long, he owed us quite a mountain of coins before Cathy declared: 'He's nithing bit a fuckin' tap, dinna you let him in again!' But Peter always made me laugh, especially when I was stoned. It wasn't that he had a great sense of humour—in fact, the poor chap was quite oblivious to how he might appear to the outside eye. It was his peculiar medley of incongruencies coupled with Cathy's sheer disgust with the man that tickled my fancy.

Meanwhile, the lodgings on West End Lane were cheap and in a great location, but they were far from perfect. With only the one bathroom on our landing, Cathy and I were often forced to pee in the kitchen sink.

'Cathy, fa' the fuck's in 'at lavvy a' this time?'

'Fuck only knows, bit I'm fucked if al be gan in 'ere ayfter 'at stench!'

'Fuckin' great! Constipated cunt.'

The sink was in a knocked-out pantry next to the gas cooker, and Mr Asher, our greedy landlord, had surrounded this 'kitchen' with three flimsy walls, to which he added a table and chairs and called it the dining room. Cathy, a couple of inches shorter than me, had to drag a wooden box over to raise her bum up to the sink—but I was by far the worst culprit.

One Sunday morning, chock-full of drink from the night before at the Leicester Square dancing, I was bleary-eyed sloshed and peeing in the sink when I realised things weren't going to end there.

'Cath? Cathy! I'm awa ti' hae a shite!' I cried out.

'No yer fuckin nae!' she commanded, and stomped into the room shaking her fist. 'Ye fool fuckin' moch, dinae' you dare shite in 'at sink!'

But then to my desperate plea of 'I canna help it, it's comin' *oot!*' she took one look at my crimson-red face and commenced holding her stomach and laughing.

'Well, I'm nae fuckin' cleaning it!'

'Geeze a bowl then, *quick!*' I begged. She passed me the soup bowl, and just like that, out with a *plip-plop* I pushed and squeezed—and 'African soup' was born!

Now Cath—in the tradition of proper Scottish hospitality—had many times offered Peter a bowl of whatever she cooked. Due to her generosity, he had sampled the finest of Scottish cuisine with umpteen bowls of broth, stovies, and even the occasional plate of mince n' tatties, our favourite in-the-money treat. Climbing down from the sink, completely exhausted by my efforts, my 'African soup' was now put under wraps on the dining room table.

'Shall we drop it down the toilet?'

'Nah, I've a better idea 'n 'at. Geeze 'at spliff.' Sure enough, by the time we'd lit and puffed on our second joint, Peter came rapping at the door, probably having smelt the aroma of cannabis from the lobby.

'Come in, Peter, have a seat, take a blow,' we said, unusually polite, handing him the joint. "There's a bowl of soup if you fancy.", The smile lighting up his greedy face dropped into stark reality when he removed the plate on top, and saw he had been served a turd in a bowl. In horror he fell backwards. Cathy and I threw ourselves on to the floor and were rolling about in hysterics when Peter stood his full height and lunged at me.

'You little minx!'

I scrambled to my feet and managed a couple of circuits around the bedsit before I finally dodged him and legged it out the door.

'Run, Vic!'

There was nowhere to run though, and he was hot on my tail: 'I'll spank your bottom, you naughty girl!' Desperate, I stumbled into the Irish room for safety—yet even that failed to stop Peter. He bombed in after me and in this room—a good bit smaller than ours—he cornered me and dragged me on to the already occupied settee, then pulled me over his knee, lifting my hippy skirt over my bare bum and proceeding to give me six of the best. 'Why you—*whaaack!*—filthy little madam!—*whaaack*—you naughty, naughty girl!—*whaaack!*'

It was only when the punishment was over, and I lifted my head ready to let him have it, that I noticed my friends' faces white with shock. I surveyed the scene, surprised to find sitting on the best chair next to the fireplace sipping tea out of their best cup and saucer their dog-collared guest, the chaplain, who had finally taken up their invitation to pop in for Sunday tea!

'Fuuuuuck, so sorry,' I gulped.

'Erm … hmm well, well, what a pleasant surprise,' coughed and sputtered Peter. He patted me playfully on the bum, sliding his hand into his pocket, then turned to the chaplain. 'More tea, Vicar?'

'Surely,' replied the chaplain, raising his cup. 'Don't mind if I do.'

Such were the naughty pranks of West End Lane.

Yet there was another side to it. Things I would recognise later as symptomatic of tragedy or trauma from the past—for instance, the mood swings I'd had since puberty—were dealt with now without question. During one of my downers, Cathy and I would go to the off-licence for sherry, stay at home and get drunk for a few days, and then that was that; life would be happy again. It wasn't a topic up for discussion. I'd just say, 'Cathy, do you fancy getting a few bottles of sherry in?' and she'd go up to Stanley's Stores at the top of the hill. No questions were ever asked, nor objections raised.

Dope was another pastime during those early years.

I loved it at first, especially because Cathy was so entertainable. I used my acting and posing skills to give her good or bad trips, pretending to be at the carnival, getting her higher and higher then suddenly changing to a cackling witch or bloodthirsty vampire and freaking her out until she begged me to stop.

'FER FUCK'S SAKE STOP! ENOUGH, YER FREAKIN' ME OOT!'

'Okay, okay, sorry! I wis only hay'in a laugh!'

'WELL, YE KIN FUCK RIGHT OFF WI' YER JOKES, YE FUCKIN' WEIRDO!'

Sometimes we made fairy cakes and offered them to our neighbours. Not the Irish girls—we knew our boundaries—but we did include the local bobby, and there were many marijuana-filled nights when I entertained the audience dancing with his truncheon. 'PC Plod', as we called him, was a lovely guy and became one of my dearest friends. Other evenings, Barry—once a mercenary, now a London Underground train driver who drowned his war memories with alcohol—told us tales of hiking through the jungle, stories that always ended with him staggering to his feet and growling ape-like as he chased some imaginary foe.

Then there was the young Arab who hung around our garden. I thought he was peeping at first, but when confronted it turned out he was having a fly smoke away from his uncle's gaze. No problem—now we had a paying customer. The Arab would tell his undoubtedly mega-rich uncle he was going to the barber, and the price of a haircut became his £20 'entrance fee'.

The first time we entertained him with our exotic belly dance and gave him a trim, but it fell into a routine rental for letting him hang out and have a smoke inside—not bad when our actual weekly rent was only £14. It was a time when London was filled with rich Arabs in chauffeur-driven rollers or strolling along Oxford Street dishing out £50 notes as tips. We'd all heard the stories, but tales of rich sugar daddies didn't interest me. I knew what I wanted, and all things considered £20 was a good deal. Such was our life and whatever else our housemates may have thought of us, we certainly brought the place together and brightened it up. It was a good time, full of new experiences. We were skint but full of dreams and good old-fashioned belly laughs.

The biggest dream of all was becoming a professional model. The nudes I had done up until now were 'safe nudes'—those that would never be published. The soft porn I did was only on Polaroid or in private shows for voyeurs—'the dirty raincoat brigade', as us girls called them. I had been advised that if I wanted to be in advertising, on Page 3 and the covers of magazines, I should avoid showing more than boobs in publications. I'd heard whispers of girls losing their agents because photos of them had been uncovered in a 'Swedish mag', that sort of thing. In those days, the only true porn stars were the men. Linda Lovelace's fame was, sadly, about what she did rather than who she was, and there were no role models for us glamour girls beyond the vagina-less statuesque art model relics from the 1960s and the pre-Samantha Fox girl next doors in *The Sun*, who were just a tad too posh to have that many neighbours.

This was the modelling world I knew from about 1976 to 1978.

Then I met Mr Dudley. I will always remember his genteel demeanour. He wore a trilby hat and a raincoat with a brown leather briefcase perched on his knees, his highly polished shoes shining under neatly pressed turn-ups. Mr Dudley was quite old; his skin already had that translucent glow and his facial muscles had begun gently hanging, but as with everything else about him, completely inoffensively. He had the warmest of smiles and the kindest of eyes.

After a moment of sitting opposite me on the train, he uttered the classic pickup line: 'Are you a model?' Rolling my eyes in a way he thought was attractive, I affirmed that I was. It turned out that Mr Dudley was a member of Clapham Camera Club—a club that was quite renowned for housing some decent amateurs and being a stable from which many a hopeful young girl found fame and fortune. I hoped to be one of them.

Accepting his invitation, I was added to The List. I posed for 'Dudley', as I came to call him. Not sure I would call him a friend, but he was certainly a mentor. Cathy had dubbed him Dudley out of disrespect, claiming he was a disgusting dirty old man—but the name hadn't come across like that, it suited him, and I kept it. Even though I once visited his semi in Uxbridge to pose for him, Dudley never revealed much about his life. I knew he was a widower; I'd heard he was a retired civil servant. That was all he gave away. I wondered sometimes if he'd worked for MI5; I could see him secluded in the shadowy back office of a 007 movie.

That said, there could be, and very often was, a deep respect and love between photographer and model. The same was true model to model. It was something the outside world would never see or understand. The interpretations and projections that can be attached to someone like me are quite incredible. I know now that those projections are about the person projecting, but back then I internalised them as being unpopular, unworthy, disliked, not good enough. Cathy's disrespect for Dudley and others like him fed a silent embryo inside me that had been growing there for a long time.

* * *

'Snelling is smelling in the middle of the spelling …'

The schoolgirl voices sang, haunting me over the years, echoing behind the unspoken pictures in my mind. I'd been born Vicki Snelling; that translated into 'Smelling' in the cloakroom of my posh girl's school. I remember endless playtimes standing alone, staring sadly out from under the laburnum tree feeling worse than awful. I believed I was smelly, although try as I might, I couldn't smell myself. I knew I had frizzy hair and probably bad breath—my mother had bad breath, and I must have it too. My legs were shorter than everyone else's—I knew that because I had painstakingly done the ratios. I wished I had the ever-popular yellow-blonde Barbie doll hair, got invited to all the parties, that my uncle was a famous footballer, and I could be on an ice cream advert like one of the girls in my class. My mother was a liar saying I was bonny. Shame and fury snowballed from her lie. I hated that school, and I hated my mum and dad for making me go there.

Repeating the shame by using my birth name in my new calling would only open me to further ridicule.

Yet here I was: destiny's moment had arrived, and Mr Dudley, very proud, had 'discovered' me.

'What name do you go by?' he inquired.

'Er …,' I stuttered, mind reeling. I felt the blood draining from my brain. 'Vicki …,' I finally stammered out, catching my breath. 'Vicki Scott.'

'Vicki Scott. Fine,' Mr Dudley replied, taking my arm. 'Shall we visit my club then, Miss Vicki Scott?'

Camera Clubs paid £5 an hour—not hugely exciting, but I had my steady work at Miss Candy's, and I'd learnt a lot: make-up, lighting, which clothes to bring, what poses worked, which ones did not. There was a set routine, from everyday shots through bikini shots to the very classical nudes: knees firmly together. I remember lugging a massive suitcase up West End Lane onto the Tube, changing at Oxford Circus for Victoria, then staggering to the overground train for the couple of stops to Clapham Junction, slogging up that hill and trudging up the stairs …

All for a fiver!

It was through the Camera Club circuit that I began meeting other models. We'd exchange numbers and tell each other about jobs on the go. One day I got a call: 'There's a job in South London, you'll need to take the overground train; it's just girl-on-girl posing for a guy who likes to watch, there's no film in the camera.'

My face collapsed. *Girl-on-girl?*

I had done lots of girl-on-girl stuff—soft porn, play-acting sex really. I would not have described them as lesbian experiences, just acting it out with my mates. But the pay was good—quite good, actually. So off I went on the train overland, heading further south than ever before. I was wearing a new acquisition, a beautiful trench coat that snatched my waist, tiny from the black bombers I was picking up in Harley Street, a contact made courtesy of a new modelling friend.

Arriving, I knocked on the door of a big ground-floor flat—though it might have been a squat, when I think about it now. Big bay windows, full of Eastern shawls and tapestries, reeking of incense, and in true 1970s style, beads hanging from the door frames. The door was opened by a teensy waiflike woman with shaved red hair and several piercings. I remember thinking: 'Fuck, is she a dyke?' Her slim figure was wrapped in a Japanese kimono, and clearly nothing else. She smelled good, like she'd just climbed out of a bath steeped in exotic perfume. She smiled and pointed: 'The guy's in there.'

Hesitant, I crept into the main room. 'The guy' was sitting on a dining room chair near the fireplace, facing the single bed that was pushed against the wall as if he was about to pull it up and eat his dinner from it. 'No film' was right—there was no fucking camera!

'Well, don't just stand there! Go change!' the red-haired woman ordered me. So off to the bathroom I trudged and took all my clothes off, donning the satiny robe she tossed me. 'Now lie on the bed,' she snapped brusquely as I returned to the living room. *Lie on the bed?* It felt weird, surreal. Being the good sport, I lay on the bed, while she knelt at the other end, and the punter pulled his chair right up.

Hearing the chair screech closer, I took a peek, my eyes widening. The guy was wearing a raincoat! Not a smart one like Dudley's, though. It was huge, oversized. He sat stock-still, hairy hands clutched in his pockets. It could have been scary, only he was the one who looked terrified. Plus, he was such a scrawny weed of a man it didn't even cross my mind to be scared.

On the silent call of 'action', the redhead stretched over and undid my dressing gown, then started kissing me. 'Ooh, wait, what …?' Softly on my mouth and down my neck she went, kissing my throat, my shoulders, my bust—even how she kissed my boobs was different. I had no experience in the finer arts of lovemaking. My teenage sex life consisted of a guy squeezing your tits, poking your fanny, then shagging you. But now the way she touched my breasts gently, teasingly, opened a new world.

Suddenly I started to get feelings down between my legs. *What's this tingling?* I wondered. I remember thinking, *Oh my God, it can't be, I'm a Lizzy!* It was a flash of a thought that I didn't allow to grow; I dismissed it and said to myself: 'Let go, Vic, just enjoy it.'

I did.

Her tongue traced tantalisingly down my belly. I can still feel it now! I remember it every time someone runs their tongue down my tummy like that; I always come so quickly. This was a woman doing it to me like that—that slippery tongue sending twisted tangles of energy in all directions through my body, that guy clutching his fists in his pockets, watching. I got so turned on, my fanny was embarking on a new journey. It was a shock when all at once I realised: *Fuck me, I'm gonna come!* She hadn't even reached my mound yet. Her tongue was gentle, sensual, relentless, kissing and caressing my pussy softly with her lips. We all had a proper bush in those days; her tongue brushed my pubic hairs apart and my clit rose up to meet her mouth and her tongue leapt out and found the spot instantly, applying a gentle yet insistent pressure. At that moment, the dam burst. The waves beginning from the pearl at the centre of my pink surged throughout my body as her hands groped to lift my tiny buttocks to her hungry mouth. She was part of me, and she timed me with expert precision. Fucking ace!

She pulled back a little and tilted my pelvis so the guy could see me properly as she softly massaged all around my pubis, inner thighs, and bum, teasing me. I became aware of the intensity in the gent as he gazed at my fine, honey-scented cunt. My orgasm still tingling in my body, she took it, and with trailing fingers and hungry mouth extending the ecstasy, my world exploded into skyrockets.

I didn't know my body could do that. She taught it.

Mick had made me come for the first time ever. I was sixteen and we were babysitting. Lying in front of the fire after shagging me, he put his finger firmly on my clit and started rubbing it from side to side. *What's he doing? I wondered. Why isn't he poking me?* He kept going for ages, wiggling and waggling his fat finger. I was too polite to say but wondered what on earth he was up to. Eventually I gave up and left him to it and lay back.

As he continued jiggling his digit, suddenly a shivery sensation shot through me, and I climaxed. 'Oh God … Oh God, oh *Goddd!*' There was no warning, just a sudden, intense blast of orgasm. I didn't even know what it was but spent the next few years finding out. My investigation led me to self-experimentation. *Would any finger work? Would any direction do? Why didn't it work just with my finger inside? How many times could I do it in a day?* Suddenly I was horny morning, noon and night, playing with myself like a teenage boy—yet here I was, eighteen and parting men from their money like a pro. However, by now I did know what it meant to be horny and how to use it in my favour.

That day, in a South London squat, I found out so much more.

After the punter in his raincoat got his eyeful, the redhead and I lay a while together, stroking each other. Milk bottle legs was a call of shame in Scotland, and I was marvelling at just how pretty white skin could be … when panic set in. Still an Aberdonian quine at the core, my brain started rattling with fear of what lay ahead: *Fucking hell, am I actually going to have to lick her fanny now? What's it going to smell like, what's it going to taste like?* I calmed myself: *Vic, just do it like the soft porn shows, if there's something wrong or you don't like it you'll stop, because no one told you it was going to be for real or anything like that.* Mimicking what she did to me, I went down on her. The biggest surprise was that it did in fact smell different. It had never occurred to me that fannies might smell different from each other. Different pheromones, I suppose, and hers was softly spicy. Guys had told me mine smelled of honey. *They're full o' shit,* I told myself—but now I was starting to get it.

'Getting it' came slowly.

I wondered if all redheads were a little spicy, like Christmas potpourri with a subtle overtone of chocolate. Her hairs were bright red, and her lips vibrantly pink, almost orangey. I dived in; it was fine, but then my brain started yakking again: *Can I make her come? She's so experienced! How does this even work, how do I do it?* I believed she climaxed but was not entirely sure; she was quiet and there was nothing obvious to tell me. It's funny, as I have told many guys later in my life: 'If you have to ask, it didn't happen!' Then I climbed on top of her—I just wanted to. I shagged her, mound to mound. I could barely believe how much I enjoyed that! My 'beliefs' around homosexuality at the time consisted of: 'Guys shove their cocks up each other's arses, and women lick each other's fannies and fuck with dildos.' But the redhead from south of the river and I did lots of positions and it was excruciatingly horny. It surprised me just how versatile we could be—both of us were small, young and agile. That made it easy, as our bodies found a rhythm. In the moment, the silent wanker, at his dinner table of fanny smells and soft feminine moaning, was long forgotten, yet undoubtedly added a third dimension to that blissful encounter.

There were many more encounters of a blissful kind to be experienced. They were also well enough paid. With those, and my part-time shifts at Miss Candy's and the smaller jobs I did hoping they would lead to more, my bread and butter was now secure. Cathy signed on to the dole and between us we got to the point where we were paying the rent regularly; we didn't have to hide from Mr Asher anymore, the 'shoplifting' trips to Stanley's Stores were less frequent, and the three weeks where we lived off dehydrated veg and Oxo cubes were left far behind.

CHAPTER SIX

Cyril the Slobberer, and the Mayor of Chicago

As far as I was concerned, this was it: *I'd arrived!* Established as a model, comfortable in my own skin, and West Hampstead was my home—this was *bliss*. The reality was far better than the dream I had concocted all those years ago in the passenger seats of lorries rolling south. Okay, I smoked a little pot, did black bombers to keep my weight down, and drank when we went out clubbing. Yet the days of guzzling three bottles of sherry while cooped up at home in a messy bedsit went out the window, along with poor man's soup and shoplifting from Stanley's Stores.

My current paramour was a handsome male model I'd met on a Harrison Marks movie. We got on well; he was tall and pretty, with a wicked wit, but when the bold boy dared to voice his craving desire for fellatio—'Before you go out, babes'—my mischievous personality and new-found girl power was totally uncorked. Perhaps it was the way he begged and pleaded for it.

'Sure, hon,' I replied languidly, 'but only if I can tie you up first, because I'm going to suck and kiss and stroke and lick and tease you so much, you'll be begging for mercy.'

Now every woman knows that just the words *blow job* are enough to make most men go into an inanimate stupor: 'Wh-wh-*wha*' was that you said?' Secretly I grinned to myself; my promise had hit the mark. He was putty in my hands—well, perhaps not putty; in fact, he was growing into a very willing subject perched there like a doggy drooling for a biscuit.

'Down, boy, let me dress the part!' I reprimanded, as I ploughed and plundered through my selection of props.

Props—the tools of every model's trade—were stored by the bay window in a massive travel trunk. First, I needed to lug away the rather enormous tomato plants that were thriving on the light from West End Lane. Next, I folded the tablecloth—that necessitated getting on my knees. Then, to lift the massive trunk lid I needed to stretch my body up and forward while arching my back like an obedient horny little bitch. Finally, as if oblivious to my audience, I made a great pantomime of rummaging through my collection. 'Aaaahh, look at this mess! Hang on, while I do a quick inventory …' Unnecessary feather boas were chucked on the floor; superfluous wigs tossed on the bed, flimsy negligees, stray garters, and ropes of pearls that had somehow gotten stuck in the very bottom corner were flung across the room. 'Fuck off, don't need this, nor this, certainly don't need that …!' At last, I was satisfied: 'There you are! Handcuffs … hmmm, stockings … suspenders, some silken ties. That'll do.'

Sitting provocatively on the edge of the bed, posing, pouting, slowly sliding the stockings up and over my flawlessly toned, suntanned legs, I slipped my feet into the stilettos that were already waiting on the floor. Fuck I was good. 'Hurry up!' my hero pleaded. Ready, I nodded him on to the rug. 'Like this?' he dutifully asked. Poor little puppy lay there obediently as I deftly cuffed his hands behind his back—*click! clack!*—bound his feet, and tightened the ties around the cuffs for good measure. Then I gagged him. 'Heyyyyy … Nrrgggg … Whaaa …?' he whimpered.

'Now quiet, you. Let Mummy do her work!' Slowly and seductively, I dragged his drawers to his ankles and began gently stroking his belly.

'Ooh … Ah yeah … come on, babes!' he moaned through the gag.

'Wait, wait!' I announced, whirling around and reaching for my vibrator.

'You horny bitch,' he muttered grumpily, in agony. I squatted over him, bringing myself right to the edge with my favourite toy, then queening him as I came in his mouth. 'You horny fucking *bitch!* I'm so hard, babes!' the poor man squealed.

Placing a finger to my lips—'Shooosh now!' I breathily whispered—I leant back, placing the vibrator between his legs, then stood over him. I wet my lips, winked, and swivelled on my heels. Pulling my skirt down over my stocking tops, I picked up my handbag and portfolio, pouted over my shoulder and walked out the door: 'Can't be late for the audition, darling!' I cooed. I almost wet myself imagining the scene when Cathy got home at teatime as I wiggled my way up to the Tube station.

Deciding it was time to start exploring London in earnest, I made a pact with myself to say yes to every guy who asked me out to dinner—the goal being to sample cuisine from all around the world. The Aberdeen I'd left behind included a Chinese, an Indian, the Victoria Tea Rooms and the Wimpy. London had *everything!* I checked out the pubs on King's Road, Earls Court and Battersea. The famous Whiskey a Go-Go conveniently situated right across the road from Miss Candy's on Wardour Street was the venue to many of my escapades. However, the nightlife was a mere backdrop for me; my focus was strongly on my new career.

I kept myself fit, training in a West End gym with the East End boys from the sex shop. Confident enough of my income to start modestly spending, I bought new clothes, seeing that as an investment. Some were picked up from shoots and others from the trade fairs where me and my modelling buddies did promotional work to fill the gap until the next 'real' modelling job came along. I also invested in a bike from the shop a bit further up West End Lane. It was

£25—I thought long and hard about spending that kind of money, realising in the end it made sense.

I cycled around London meeting different photographers, showing my portfolio, and doing test shots. I was making contacts and honing the art of standing naked in heels for hours on end. It paid off. I started getting calls when just the right audition was happening.

Only a year after arriving in London, I made Page 3 of *The Sun*, thanks to a freelancer, Brian Anderson. I even fashioned the bikini bottom myself, out of an old pair of jeans and some string—shout-out to the High School for Girls! Brian whisked me to Brighton Beach where we spent hours creating the right combination of light, pose and girl-next-door sexy. We nailed it, and it bought me an agent—a hard-won prize for girls under five foot six who took their tops off. Luckily for me I'd managed to steer clear of men's magazines. You see it was okay to show your tits to every red-blooded *Sun* reader on the planet, but you absolutely crossed the purity line if you ever showed your punani as well. Many of us girls had nudes in the closet. Mine were safe on Polaroid and in the ethical cameras of the raincoat brigade.

Billy, my agent, had an office in Whinpol Street. He represented some other girls I knew, the best of the glamour bunch. Now I was sorted. I loved saying these five golden words: 'I'd better call my agent.' Having heard it was good to pop in to visit, I'd jump on the Bakerloo Line to Oxford Circus, climb the stairs, listen to the calls come buzzing in and enjoy the mad hum of the third-floor office. There was something nearly every day—if not a job, a casting, a couple of days as a film extra or some promotional work. Not all were exciting; in fact, some were second-rate, but they were *something*.

The main thing was: I was working as a model. A professional model.

My next big break came from another freelancer, Bill Lynch. Bill's studio was on the side street opposite Stanley's Stores. A cheeky little cockney, he'd call out 'Marilyn!' as I toddled up to the Tube on my way to some casting or another in my kitten-heeled mules, bubbly blonde hair, and cherry red lips. Not seeing it in myself beyond the blonde hair and scarlet mouth, I dismissed him as 'chatting me up'. I was wrong. Bill saw it—and when he got a contract with the East Midlands Electricity Board and persuaded me to do a test shoot, I saw it too. I had turned another corner. It took many more years before I acknowledged the other resemblances to Marilyn though—how could I? My innocence was something I never wanted to be reminded of.

That brochure was my first flash job and brought its own press coverage. Soon I was approached by a manager—'Cyril the Slobberer', as Cathy called him. The first gig Cyril landed me was the Earls Court Motor Show. It was a historic moment: topless models at the motor show had become an institution, and this was the last time it was ever going to happen at Earls Court. My photograph was smack bang on the front page of every national newspaper in the country—*fame at last!* I dizzily reckoned.

Cyril also managed Chaz Chesley and the Chessmen, and the girl band The Beguilers. One night when Cyril took me home, he tried to snog me at the front door: 'Gads ya guffy,' I hooted in my native brogue, shoving him away and disappearing through the front door. *Slam!* Little did he know who was climbing in the window later that evening …

Suddenly I understood: Chaz Chesley had laid claim to me at Earls Court. Charismatic and muscular with a trillion pieces of glittery bling around his neck, a full-length leopard skin coat flung around his shoulders courtesy of his mega-rich Swedish sugar mama, he snatched me by the hand—'It's too hot in here! Let's go somewhere and get a drink, shall we?'—guiding me through the crowds gawping at the shiny cars. We must have looked stunning together. Superficially I could have taken it that he was just minding me—intuitively I knew it was more than that. It was always that way with me and my men: instant! The creaky old sash windows on West End Lane took a bashing, as did the tomato plants and Cathy's sleep pattern, which she of course managed with her usual caustic wit: 'Darkies now, ye'll be on the game next.'

Nothing was ever planned with Chaz. He'd drive up in his Roller, rap on the window, and bark at me: 'Pretty up now, we're going out on the town!' Night's out with

Chaz usually ended as a late one at the Q Club. A lot of time was spent in bed too; long, lazy sex and listening to Chaz's tales. I loved my time with him, easy, comfortable, full of laughs. He was older and had lots of stories. He'd get one in his head—'Did I tell you about the two geisha girls? Honestly, darling!' he'd chortle with a swagger, all bundled in his greatcoat like Al Capone. Even Chaz's house fascinated me—a bedroom made for nothing else but shagging, a massive sound system, trophies of a life in show business and stories to match. Star-struck, I could read what other people thought of us in their eyes. I didn't care. 'Uptight busybodies,' I told myself. People were stupid. Chaz taught me a lot and we remained friends long after we stopped fucking.

Cyril didn't give up instantly though. Nor did he seem to care that Chaz was already in about—he just wanted some, too. His patience eventually ran out when after his umpteenth attempt at metaphorically describing the rules of the casting couch game, I refused to put out. 'How 'bout a shag just for fun then?' Sympathy shags just didn't happen in my world, no matter what the stakes. Cyril had gotten me a couple of big commercials—a massive step-up career-wise, and that came to an end with my final no to shagging. I didn't care; a manager had happened quite quickly for me. I'd heard of girls trying for years, while I hadn't even tried, plus I'd promised myself early on to live or die on my own two feet.

Dad had once said to me: 'If yer gan to dee 'at, quine, dee it right.' I guessed that was what he meant.

'If I'm going to be a whore,' I reminded myself bravely, 'I'll be a whore; fuck shagging some creep to get a job!' I was a model, and I was doing alright—'None of the other agency girls ever had a manager, even if he is a perv,' I reasoned—and besides life was fun, why would I need a slobberer hanging about telling me what to do?

Then Cupid struck.

* * *

Feeling on top of the world—successful, young, beautiful and full of fun—I was out celebrating with the flatmates at our local, The Railway on West End Lane, the fateful night I met GUY.

Our eyes met across the crowded bar: oh God, the man was attractive! Helplessly I tried to restrain myself, but it was too late. Instantly I felt the seductive pull. Guy must've felt it, too. He sidled up confidently asking me, 'What d'ya think of the band?'

'I fuckin' hate 'em,' I replied. That led to a drink and a mutual sharing of very different background stories.

Guy was a soon-to-be Chicago attorney, in London for summer school. I told him the now well-rehearsed Page 3 version of my story. 'I'm renting a flat above Stanley's Stores,' Guy announced, meaning we were virtually neighbours.

We were moving into a nice flowing chat when Cathy clocked that I had disappeared with one guy for longer than was 'allowed' on a girls' night out. She strutted over to investigate. Pulling me to one side by the elbow while giving Guy the best mate glower, she stage-whispered in my ear sarcastically: 'Yer nae gan wi' Yankee boy are ye?' Of course, I *was*. *That* accent, the unconscious arrogance, that haughty Jewish profile, dark brown eyes, lush skin tone, man body, and make-no-mistake-about-it stare—shit could have floated out of the man's mouth (and being an 'almost qualified' ambulance chaser, *probably did*), yet it was too late. I was already long gone.

Dating Guy added yet another new experience to my ever-growing list. The American dating style was something novel, and a far cry from the Scottish call to romance: 'D'ye funcy a shag?' I'd gone out with plenty of guys since I'd been in London, but none had turned my head the way Guy did. It was a combination of how smart he made himself sound and his burning ambition. 'Gonna be the mayor of Chicago one day,' he bragged, puffing his chest out, also boasting that he knew gangsters and hoodlums, famous American footballers, and had an apartment two blocks from the Playboy Building.

Other than my dearest friends, like Chaz, men had been either a ticket to something else or a temporary plaything. I enjoyed every minute with Guy. As I basked in that first summer of modelling success, it was easy to believe in fairy tales. Guy convinced me that I'd do even better in the States.

'Really?'

'Of *course,* really! You're beautiful, Vick!' I didn't take much persuading; we were in love, and I resolved to join him that winter in Chicago.

Still, there were hurdles. Although Cathy and I were managing to pay the rent now, money was not abundant, and the £260 flight to Chicago was a tad out of my reach. Plus, I'd be taking time off. Saving hadn't happened yet, that was for sure; there was no rainy-day money fund tucked away, and I was too proud to ask the obvious: 'Guy, can you help me with the ticket money?'

I was worried.

Turns out I had reason.

By this time, Miss Candy's Models had a sister-ship: Miss Candy's Escort Agency. Naively, I thought I'd try my hand at escorting to raise the extra money. I'd come from an Aberdeen on the brink of oil and gas wealth, where being an 'escort' meant accompanying some cowboy-hatted big-booted Texan to a square dance.

Deciding to ask Angie about this escorting stuff, she couldn't say it straight out as she normally would: 'This ain't a brothel, you're not working girls here, right?' Angie went ahead and organised it for me: 'Y'afta get all dolled up like a proper posh bird on a dinner date. D'ya know wha'ta mean?'

I thought so. In a flurry, I chose a dark green patterned dress that buttoned down the front, a tailored off-white wool jacket with massive shoulder pads, and huge platform-soled shoes. *This is going to be another level,* I thought to myself, applying the whore-like make-up I assumed would be expected. I puffed my hair up far beyond my usual curly mop, scooshed on some hairspray and headed for the Hilton, Park Lane.

'Can I help you?' asked the double-breasted, top-hatted doorman.

To which I proudly replied: 'I'm Vicki from Miss Candy's Escort Agency. I'm here to see the chap in Room 233.'

The doorman narrowed his beady eyes. 'We don't allow escorts in this hotel,' he soberly stated.

Oh. Was I that naive? Or had my higher self arrived in the nick of time, conjured up by that part of me that didn't really want to? I hadn't consciously thought about what might happen in Room 233; I expected it was up to me and I'd come up with some way to skank him. The doorman's response made my path clear.

I was lost in thought as I cut through the backstreets of Mayfair on to Piccadilly, heading back to Soho to chat it through with the girls over a cuppa. Okay, perhaps I'd overplayed it ... Maybe I shouldn't have been honest with the doorman, or maybe it just wasn't for me, no East Enders on the other end of a camera in the blinkin' Hilton. Just as I concluded that perhaps escorting was not what I was meant to do to raise money, I spied a pound note lying on the ground—right there on Piccadilly, of all places! Perhaps the streets of London were paved with gold after all! Either way for me it was a sign. There would be another plan, yet to be revealed.

Back at base, obviously early, hinting with a roll of my eyes that something went wrong, I kept the girls in suspense as I brewed everyone a cuppa. 'Come on, luv, stop the suspense, you're killing us!' they pleaded. Soon I had them all howling with laughter, mimicking my own wide-eyed naivety as I related the story in every gory detail, including the pound note, as if laid down by the hand of the Goddess Herself!

It was a quiet night; we stayed there chatting until closing time. The new girls, those taken on for the escort side, had my measure now, and a few weeks later, one of them—Jasmine—approached me. 'It's a huge party, you get two hundred pounds just to be there, no need to do anything more than that. If you quite fancy him and want to do extra, you can negotiate that yourself.'

Now that was more like it.

This time I did my due diligence, vowing to become a more expensive version of myself. I settled on a Grecian goddess look created with a beautiful silk diagonally-striped sleeveless top, a cream A-line skirt and tan heels. It was more careful, subtler than before; twin hair combs tamed my wild mop, with the final touch a beautiful gold belt I'd picked up at one of the trade fairs. Fashioned like a snake, its open mouth clasped the tail that draped beautifully below my waist, enhancing my slim hips and a skirt that clung in all the right places. Satisfied, I strolled on to West End Lane and flagged a black cab.

But my God! When I arrived at the elegant Georgian house in Knightsbridge—with decor I was frightened to touch—I felt unworthy, unfit, out of my depth. My carefully chosen attire was nothing compared to the designer outfits that fell from the shoulders of the professional courtesans in that room. *Clearly this is a case of invest for success,* I told myself. These women weren't as beautiful as I imagined they would be—not like models—yet they were engaging, interacting, softly giggling and hanging on to every word of whomever they conversed with. Meanwhile, I went into a complete panic. I froze, overwhelmed by feelings of shyness, incompetence, ineptitude, illiteracy. *What the fuck, what now, holy moley! What am I supposed to do, who was I meant to talk to?* One or two guys gave me the eye as I wandered around awkwardly, but they weren't that interested. Why would they be? I was such an oddball!

Am I supposed to make the move? I wondered. *Perhaps if I tried an encouraging look on top of my traumatised, not-good-enough face.* Fat fucking chance. I felt like running away—scared, unworthy and tongue-tied. None of the girls looked friendly either, and quickly looked away when I tried to make eye contact. *Stuck-up cows. Bunch of fuckin' hookers anyway.* I was back in the playground of that posh school again, for fuck's sake!

Eventually I spotted sanctuary: an empty chair at the dinner table near a window. *Fabulous! I'll just sit here and mind my own.* Escape was probably the best option, and just as I was wondering how long I'd have to stay to earn my two hundred, I noticed out of the corner of my eye an Arab gazing across at me. *Was there a skinny bitch behind me taking his attention?*—no, every time I glanced over, he was definitely staring. Sitting on one of the silk and mahogany sofas by the fireplace, dressed in traditional Arabic thobes, he was no da Vinci oil painting. In fact, I think he fell off the ugly tree and hit every branch on the way down. Slightly chubby with an unfortunate underbite, my admirer's eyes remained warm and understanding. *That'll do.*

He beckoned me over.

After exchanging pleasantries, he delivered the classic: 'What's a nice girl like you doing in a place like this?'

I sighed. *Abdul, the Bahraini businessman to the rescue, send in the cavalry, t'rin t'rin ta'rin tin tin.* No reason to lie, I blurted out, 'I want money for my flight to Chicago so I can go live with my boyfriend this winter.'

For a moment Abdul looked traumatised. 'Why's he not paying for it?' he asked—*fair point.*

'Oh, he's a student, studying to be a lawyer,' I said, embarrassed, wondering to myself why *wasn't* Guy paying for it? It was true, he was a student, but hadn't he said his apartment lay only two blocks from the Playboy Building? And what about that mega allowance from the parents? Anyway, after hearing me blab on, Abdul offered the flight money—*nice one!* There was an honesty in his jolly face and a twinkle in his eye that told me he knew fine what I was up to, that I was 'naughty', but that I didn't have to be with him.

'These are not nice girls here,' he said. *You're telling me, mate—stuck-up whores and a half!* The implication was that I was a nice girl, and that was how he'd like me to stay—*Okay then!* So, when he said we'd have to go to his hotel room for the flight money, I checked in on the nerves in my belly … *It would be alright,* came the reply, so why not, let's go along with it and see.

And it was fine. We ordered room service, had more chat, normal everyday chat, unlike the code talk at the party, which was way beyond me and seemed like some secret society bullshit. Abdul seemed simple and direct in the same way as I had always been. He had a cute, childish sense of humour, which I didn't mind at all—*A simple bastard,* I realised—and we had some laughs. He named me Miss Piggy, told me not to do dirty things—*As if,* I giggled—gave me the £260 for the flight, some spending money and sent me home in a cab. Result! No kisses, no nothing! Not even a hint of it!

It was the beginning of a seven-year-long affair with a man who became not only my sugar daddy, but one of my closest friends.

And, I had my ticket to Chicago.

* * *

I arrived at O'Hare on a bitter cold November morning just after I turned twenty-one, Guy's 'foxy babe' dressed in skin-tight jeans, over-the-knee striped socks, pale blue beret, and a purple feather earring. This was brand new. I couldn't wait.

Chicago was a disappointment—an utter, freezing, impenetrable, disappointment. Playboy Agency went no further than an interview. I couldn't get to grips with the 'Have a nice day' culture—what was wrong with these people? Disillusioned, I went clothes shopping and found the women all utterly obsessed with the size on the label. And Guy's friends were ALL Jewish. I didn't mind the Jews, but there must be something well wrong with him that he didn't have one single goy friend!

Well, let me correct that: when we went out to a nightclub, he acted like he was friends with the Black footballers. However, I could tell they thought he was a cunt, shaking their hands and acting like they were long lost 'brothers'. He used to say to the valet boys: 'Flip my lid and pick my 'fro,' as if he had some street cred—they thought he was a cunt, too.

I also started to understand why there was never even a visit of acknowledgement from his stoically Jewish parents. His mates cracked Gentile jokes all the time. I was starting to think I was the stupid shiksa shag who'd paid for her own ticket to come to the bloody Windy City for a using. PLUS, I was getting impatient for the ring he promised, *Mayor of Chicago's wife* ...

I was starting to think that he was a cunt, too.

The worst of it all was that I was bored. *I Dream of Jeannie* reruns and Americanised versions of TV snacks didn't quite cut it. I rang Abdul—'Will ye front me another ticket? I'm fallin' apart here!'—no point in having a cavalry without blowing the bugle now and then.

When the money arrived, I packed my black Samsonite and left. *Adios amigo!*

* * *

On 23 December 1977, New York was white with snow. Just like in the movies, the shoppers on Fifth Avenue had their arms full of beautifully wrapped gifts. It was enchanting. I loved it. Abdul had sent me two grand—plenty to treat myself and take plentiful gifts home to the family.

I asked the stewardess on the flight where they stayed and checked in there. That night I tasted my first oysters and sat at the beautiful piano bar deliciously alone, sipping Martinis—another first—and daydreaming that life was going to be amazing. It hurt a little; he'd tried to use me. I had loved him, at first anyway, but there was more for me than waiting for some guy to make up his mind. I made it home to Scotland in time for Christmas; I'd never been so glad to see my family, even my silly little sisters. They were all happy to see me too—'Far ye been, sis? Go on, tell us, was it exciting, fit did ye buy, show us yer claes?'—and not for the last time I appreciated our straightforward couthy ways. I was so glad I was Scottish and so happy to be home.

Back in London, the morning sickness began. The big boobs and passing out in Lisle Street Deli while out for my liver paté and pickle sandwiches were all Angie needed to flag it up: 'You sure you ain't preggers, luv?'

she inquired. I called Mum and Dad from the phone booth in West Hampstead station.

'We canna hear ye, quine, far are ye? Fit ye deein'? Fit happened? Jesus bloody Christ, ye better spik ti yer da.'

Dad was the wise one. I wanted a future. There was only one choice. Not so much for my Irish Catholic girlfriend, Antoinette, though. Cathy hadn't been much interested; we were growing apart. Cathy had always been hell-bent on finding someone to put a ring on her finger. It seemed my recent successes had driven her to the point where she couldn't abide listening to my romantic tales and gave little more than a caustic: 'Fuck's sake, ye stupid cunt, a telt ye nae ti ging wi' him' in response to my plight. Was she starting to hate me?

Tears pricking my eyes, I wandered up West End Lane to Antoinette and Larry's. They had moved into the flat on top of Stanley's Stores—their first proper home together. Antoinette took one look at my face, sent Larry to the pub, and got the bottle of sherry out. I told my tale of woe as we slowly got drunk: 'Jaysus, Mary Mother of God, ye have to at least tell him, he might want it, you have to gi' him the chance!'

'I don't know, Ant.' I sighed. 'He told me his last bit o' stuff had an abortion.'

'*Holy Jaysus!*' She crossed herself furiously. 'Jist as well he's not here, now if I got me hands on him …' Eventually she convinced me: 'Look let's jist go to the phone box, if he won't do the right thing by ye, he can burn in the fires o' hell.'

So it was in the early hours of the morning, armed with a bag full of coins, propping me up as I sniffled and sobbed my way along, she pushed me into the first functioning phone booth we could find. It wasn't easy getting through to America—'Operator, long distance please, I need to speak with a man in Chicago'—but we did.

Biting my nail and my lip, I blurted the news straight out. Guy replied in kind: 'Go tell the Arab.'

Click!

The wind around the phone booth let out a piercing growl. For a split second I thought I was going to burst into tears. Instead, I kept biting my lip and trembling like a child. Finally, I hung up the phone and hugged Antoinette, as the wind died outside. A few days and £200 later, it was all over, and as I lay on that clinic bed, I knew something had died inside, too.

CHAPTER SEVEN

Alter Egos and the Naked Bush

For Vicki, 1978 was a time of moving on. The Scottish friends said goodbye to the Irish sisters, to West End Lane, to a time of innocence, and to each other.

Heartache had resolved into determination, and Vicki ramped up her efforts to fulfil her dream of being an actor and comedienne. She performed extra work, made TV appearances and commercials; she appeared in several saucy British movies, including The Bitch with Joan Collins. Vicki always made time for the press and continued doing test shots. She registered with new talent agents, and saw an increase in her advertising work, both as herself and as a Monroe lookalike. She found it strange walking into auditions with her two portfolios: 'This is me, and this is Marilyn,' and then being chosen to play her alter ego, or at least a version thereof. She invested in a handmade Marilyn wig and outfits made by a seamstress specialising in stage clothing for drag artists: two copies of the white New York subway classic, the gold evening dress, the sequins and feather number Marilyn *and Jane Russell wore in Gentlemen Prefer Blondes, and the Bus Stop outfit. She soon gained a reputation for being the best Monroe lookalike of her era. Indeed, Vicki felt a great affinity with the late star, having left her own Norma Jean behind in Chicago and having a behind-the-scenes dalliance with drugs and depression.*

One article at the time told the story this way:

Under five-and-a-half feet and blonde, Vicki Scott has a body which is neat and firm and yet soft with a particular appeal: being vulnerable while at the same time just giving the impression of being at her peak, in her prime. This fruitiness, ripe and ready for the picking, was a quality Monroe had ... She may not appear as much like Monroe as some of the other lookalikes ... but in transposing her specific and prurient quality into the Monroe outfits she has become the successful one.

[Talking about Miss Candy's] she seemingly unconsciously gives a radiant smile: 'I thought this was modelling stardom not knowing anything about it ...

Her smile is sweet; a soft mouth and good teeth draw you in as you talk to her. It's seductive in the Marilyn Vein, an appeal which is unaware of itself, yet very aware—the more so when she is being photographed. She is completely at ease with her body, undressing in front of us as if it were the most natural thing when journalists call. It would be ridiculous to be coy. When she poses, she changes position effortlessly and positively, as if there is no other way possible to be photographed.

This was the Vicki who rented her first 'proper' flat. The first-floor, one bedroom, at 35 St Paul's Avenue, Willesden Green, with her own bedroom, kitchen and bathroom, and the deal-clinching circular dining table in the bay window. Breakfast was her favourite time to sit there gazing out into the quiet safety of suburbia. Having laid out her mammoth selection of marmalades and jams—a novelty that stayed with her for many years after first being able to afford it—Vicki'd watch the trees, the cats and the occasional old lady walking to the shops, while serving herself endless rounds of slightly burned toast and strongly brewed pots of tea while she made her 'calls'.

'Willesden Green 2' was the first time she'd ever decorated; the living room had a wall of chocolate brown hessian wallpaper, a coffee table, and the best brown velvet bed settee Selfridges could offer. She'd often walk to the shops at the top of St Paul's Avenue with her black cat, Jock, perched on her shoulder.

* * *

As I look back, I see that phase of my life as a time of numbness and confusion. Had there been another set of players on the stage, it could have been a time of healing and of great success. I remember the satisfaction of knowing I was a proper professional model; I loved that. The awkward, heavily accented, slightly chubby-faced me was gone. My face had slimmed down. I made sure my body stayed slim, as I could afford the hours of looking after myself, and I was beginning to develop good taste in clothes and a style I could call my own.

Outwardly successful, inwardly hurt, I'd buried the hurt from Guy deep, but not from Cathy. Cathy had found love in a tall, handsome Kiwi called Dale and moved to Shepherd's Bush with him. She should have been—and I believe she was—happy, yet sadly I saw no sign of her wanting to share that happiness with me. It was this type of sister-wound that seemed to follow me all my life.

When Cathy left, she closed a door on me, and I couldn't understand why. There was plenty she could complain of; I'd always fallen short on my share of the cooking and cleaning—'Fit's adee wi you that ye canna sweep ayfter ye mak crumbs? Ye've dribbled yer soup a'wey. An' fit—ye too good to flush the lavvy ayfter ye hae a shite now?—ye, fool fuckin' moch, fuckin' useless!' On the other hand, I'd always made sure she was included in my escapades and helped her along in many other ways. In fact, Cathy had opportunities because of me that she never would have found herself. Yet I sensed a resentment from her and had no idea where it came from.

Now she was not only with a boyfriend—a department she had struggled in—but a great one. Dale was good-looking; he dreamed of being an actor one day. Despite them being such an odd couple, he adored her. He was popular with all the guys he worked with in the sex shop downstairs: Captain Kirk, Kenny the Milk Tray Man, the Brothers Glid. They were a great bunch, hard boys who didn't suffer fools gladly, unapologetically brimming with youthful self-confidence.

Being part of a couple had clearly boosted Cathy's confidence too and had given her a sense of belonging around Candy's—yet it was equally clear that I was not to be part of that growth. Did she feel that I had been in the way before? I asked if anything was wrong: a tight-lipped 'No' was the reply. An obvious lie! She'd drawn a line, and that was that. I was locked out. I'd shared all my ups and downs with her, her family had always welcomed me when I went through hard times at home and without Cathy, without our far-from-saintly sisterhood, I felt lonely and alone. It wasn't that I struggled for company—it just wasn't the same as having someone who'd been there with me through it all, and as I met new friends, I always had the feeling that each new relationship was temporary. It left me feeling more alone than ever. Sinking into despair, I loved my cat a lot.

Cathy wasn't the only girlfriend to turn her back on me; Fiona had, too.

Fiona Rattray was from a huge family who owned the first colour TV on her street. She was almost a year older than I was, taught me about make-up, and had a crush on my dad. 'Ooh, he's handsome for an *older man!*' she whispered.

Dad noticed of course—not much went past him: 'Stupid bugger,' was his response to an eyelash flapping session. ''At lassie's nae right in the heid, quine, you watch yersel wi' her.' Fiona seemed very grown-up to me; yet, yes, she was strange.

Fiona was my pre-Cathy bestie. Not long after we met Cathy, Fiona got serious with her boyfriend, and we didn't see so much of her. After they broke up, Fiona came to visit us in London, had a brief affair with an Arab businessman, returned to Scotland, met her future husband, wrote to tell me the news, and then never spoke to me again. This was the part I could never get my head around. *What've I done? Whatever it is, why don't they just come out n' say it?*

I remember my middle sister once declaring to me, 'You're selfish.'

'What do you mean exactly?' I asked.

'You're a selfish cunt,' she replied. End of conversation. Stunned, I tried to remain philosophical. How could I amend what I could not see myself, and no one could be bothered to explain?

The camaraderie of the girls at Miss Candy's did make up in part for the lack of a close friend. I enjoyed them, each one travelling from another place to find fortune on the mean streets of London. The culture and the hurts they had left behind peeked through the curtains in what they chose for their lunchtime sandwich, how they spent Christmas and New Year holidays, their ideals and their starry dreams about the future.

Alter egos abounded everywhere.

There was Janet with the ruby-red bipolar lips that either could curl up into an alluring smile, bringing with it the sparkle of blue-grey eyes outlined by black lashes and brows, or into a downward twist, a vixen snarl, which easily sent uncooperative punters shuffling down the stairs and uninitiated colleagues scurrying to the kettle in the corner. Her bank teller husband, whom I only caught a glimpse of once or twice, was the cowering Tim to Janet's dominant hand. I have always wondered at the conversation that took that pair to the streets of Soho:

'Are ye serious? It's fuckin' *horrible* there!'

'What's so horrible about it?'

'Seven different kinds of dogshit on the pavement!'

'Oh, so you're a woman o' the world are ye now? Get yerself over here!'

'Get your hands off me!'

I have no doubt they ended up together in a comfortable suburb far away from either Soho or the Blarney Stone. Janet herself had a daytime office job, one her broad hips and plain-ish brown hair seemed far more suited to than the seedy Soho studio where we met. Yet there she was, unspoken second in command, one more alter ego that had found its home at Candy's. Certainly, her returning group of clients never took anyone *but* Janet and whatever it was that she served upstairs in her lilting Irish way.

Then there was Lolita, with the light grey eyes and pouty burgundy lips, and the longest legs I've ever seen. Lolita's long black hair kept in short bangs at the front, tied up in a ribbon in the midsection, then left to flow free down her back, with the ever-present denim shorts and flat shoes, personified her schoolgirl charm. However, it was her only play and as cute as Lolita was, it turned out she was much less popular than I would have guessed. Her heart wasn't in it; it turned out she was using smack and living in a South London squat. She wandered in and out of Candy's, never spoke of home, and one Christmas when I asked, denied its very existence.

Bridget was not unlike her namesake, Bardot, her hair a dirtier blonde and her eyes a greyer blue. Still, she was half French, and as exotic as we had at the time. Like Lolita, Bridget's allure was not universal, but she did alright when no one better was around.

Those were the main players at a time when life, as it does, turned another corner.

I had been stepping away from Candy's as more professional work came in. Thus, I wasn't aware of exactly how it started, but Cathy—now calling herself 'Catherine'—was becoming an indispensable feature around the place. Angie experienced health problems that kept her at home, so Catherine was on. She ran the place well; however, my chin dropped the first time I saw her take a punter upstairs and registered the coy look she threw me over her shoulder. Who was this woman? I'd known her for eight years, tried to encourage her in every possible way, urged her to just take an easy punter—'Maybe one who insists only on you, what d'ye think?' I suggested. I absolutely believed there was no way in the world she would ever expose her fanny to the lens, but there she was, ascending the stairs with a spring in her step, one eyebrow raised, the irresistible sex goddess.

Watching this, I felt the blood draining from my brain. *What could have happened in Shepherd's Bush that convinced Catherine to expose her naked bush?* The confidence that comes from being loved, perhaps; I never found that out for sure. Our closeness had gone, never to return. It wasn't the first time in my life, and it certainly wouldn't be the last, that I had been the catalyst for someone else's growth—the final step of which was for them to somehow annihilate me, the living reminder of a distasteful step they felt they'd taken along the way.

That summer Catherine was at Candy's a lot, doing photo work upstairs. Despite—or maybe because of—the growing distance between us, she gave me the shout when some fellow Aberdonians came looking for me. 'Curly 'n 'em were in lookin' for ye; they're at the pub 'roon the corner waiting.' I reeled, trying to catch my breath. Why was *I* getting them? She was no less connected. Was she doing me a favour? Or was she getting rid? Whatever! They all ended up back at my place and I woke up the next day with Curly in my bed, someone else moaning on the floor, and the proverbial 'What happened?' spiralling through my mind.

Certainly, I was surprised to find Curly in bed with me! This was no head-over-heels affair. He was someone I'd known forever, didn't have any feelings like that for, and concluded that I must have fallen asleep drunk. However, he was still there the next night—and something *did* happen. Still, when the gossip broke that he'd left his girl in Baker Street for me, I wasn't happy about it. Everyone at home knew I had made Page 3. My celebrity had been confirmed when my sister overheard two teenage boys sitting behind her on the double decker going into town: 'Have you seen Vicki Scott in *Men Only*, she's fae Northfield ye ken,' one asked.

'Aye, she's one o' the Snelling quines, I've shagged her!' the other bragged in response.

We did the maths; he would have been all of six when I last lived in Aberdeen! Knowing perfectly well that I was now the famous Aberdonian with her own place in London, that 'Jimmy' would score brownie points just by having paid me a visit, I was concerned that Curly had just traded up without even asking. I was also a tad guilty. I didn't need or want to steal someone else's boyfriend; he'd just wormed his way into my bed and stayed there.

This was the part of me that had become numb. A year or two earlier, Cathy would have made sure these wankers weren't invited back, and Curly would have ended up on the same slag heap as Cyril. Now, I simply remember having a gnawing feeling that this was not a good move. I hadn't chosen this, but the more I thought about it, the more I tried to figure it out, the more confused I became. In the end, I simply registered my displeasure, stating the obvious through clenched teeth:

'You know you're not my boyfriend, right?'

After a long, embarrassed pause he walked away. That was it.

That numb confusion stayed with me throughout the subsequent five years, as Curly floated in and out of my life and beyond. Not having the right ears to hear my deepest pain and vexed by my single-minded determination to 'carry on regardless' left me vulnerable, groomed, open to relationships that simply were not good for me for a long, long time.

Yet my relationship with Curly did hold some solace—if not in his arms, it was in the comfort of our tribal connection, the ability to lapse into Doric and the knowing that came from having run those backstreets together. Small and skinny with a slightly lame arm, Curly somehow managed cute and feisty. Over time I developed an admiration for the confidence he seemed to dredge up from nowhere. Curly hadn't had a good start in life, yet brass-necked his way into many more beds than just mine. He reminded me of Dustin Hoffman in *Midnight Cowboy*. While it was a relationship without passion it was also without pain; we let each other get on with our lives. Friends with benefits in the late 1970s were introduced as: 'Oh that's just Curly,' as if the name itself ought to explain his status.

He did take advantage, though; it wasn't long before his cousin came down for a visit from Aberdeen and the two gave me my first fix.

We were sitting in the lounge of St. Paul's Avenue when the discussion of heroin came up. I asked all the questions, as neither of them looked in a bad way from it, not nodding off or drooling or looking half-dead like the scary stoners I'd seen hunched on street corners—in fact they made it sound great. 'It'll go straight to your brain and feel like an orgasm spreading all over your body,' I was told, in glittery terms. Persuaded, I pushed my sleeve up; Curly did the rest. Instantly a flare of intense physical arousal mushroomed in my brain. Like some long-lost lover coming home, heroin filled all the emptiness there had ever been, slaked a thirst I didn't know I'd had, and left me wanting no more than to sit silently in its euphoric embrace.

Like most addicts, I didn't believe addiction would happen to me. At first, heroin—both my painkiller and my caffeine—Curly, and the taste of wealth I was already enjoying, simply spurned me on. Professionally there was no stone left unturned. I took jobs I had previously turned my nose up at and morphed into 'Vicki Scott, well-known soft porn model in the 1970s and 1980s'. I became Abdul's lover, travelled to meet him in Paris, Geneva and his homes in Bahrain and Abu Dhabi. In those days it was easy to pop some smack inside and go through Heathrow unquestioned.

Looking back, I remember very little of our personal life. Curly treated my place as home: we shared my breakfast routine like an old married couple, he knew my wardrobe well enough to make suggestions for a special date or audition, and exactly how long to clear off for when I'd had enough of him:

'Fit now—ye got yer chatties or somethin', woman?'

'Ahh, fuck off, ye creep!'

'Still, one o' the girls will be lookin' for a score fae "Paddington Bear"!'

'Fuck off 'n stop makin' me sick—Paddington-fuckin'-Bear my arse!'

His own life outside of St. Pauls Avenue, as far as I knew, consisted of scoring for and getting blow jobs from the working girls, a little shoplifting when he had to, but mostly ducking and diving around Paddington. We didn't make plans, just had spates of being together, when Curly was down on his luck, or I was desperate for a score.

Scoring from Curly meant *sharing* with Curly, so I avoided it as much as possible. When I did, it often meant a visit to Annie—another Aberdonian—and her man, Ari from Palestine, in their squat down the back of Maida Vale. They were professional shoplifters. They nearly always had good gear, decent brown I can still taste to this day. I remember sitting on one of the cushions strewn around the floor then sinking back while the drug slithered down my spinal column, surrendering to the incense, throws and warmth of the softly candlelit world Annie and Ari had created. Ari was a great cook, whom I credit with opening my taste buds to Middle Eastern cuisine. I was astounded by how they managed all of that in a squat and with a habit several years further down the road to ruin than mine.

The four of us were close and I enjoyed the unspoken connection we shared. However, the harsh light of morning showed a different reality. The cold unkempt toilet, towels I was never quite sure about using, Annie and Ari reluctantly heading out for their day shoplifting—'Shall we try the record shop on Broadwick Street, luv? Keen to try the new pocket you sewed into my coat?'—while Curly and I headed home for tea, toast, the rest of our score and a warm bed. Heroin didn't rule my life—not yet—and after a couple of days getting stoned and watching videos, I would start to get bored and feel my other life calling. I wanted to get back to work and kick Curly out.

Although I didn't realise it at the time, life would have become one-dimensional very quickly if I had done otherwise.

There was another part of me growing at that time, too. I was becoming a new person in a new world, in awe of the universe around me, discovering the deep intensity and passion of my sexual nature as I moved into womanhood, on my own terms.

CHAPTER EIGHT

Pearl the Trucker

A s I sit here writing, sipping chai, drinking in the sweet scent of jasmine that haunts South India, I remember a working girl I once knew. Like her namesake, she was sweet and delicate, with tiny features, light brown curly hair, and the softest jade green eyes I'd ever seen. Always an enigma: never a coarseness, a sign of being battered, bruised, or abused; any shadows from the past that had led Jasmine were pushed deep. A true angel of the night.

* * *

Jasmine and I became friends around the time I found that pound note on Piccadilly. She and Caine—her strong, muscular, sexy lover—invited me to a party. 'It's at our place in Cricklewood, you will be coming, won't you, darling?' It was my first experience of London's West Indian party scene: bodies swaying to reggae and soul, erotic and raw, packed into two ganja-filled rooms. Everyone looked so comfortable, at ease, so into it—as if they had connected with the secret hum of the universe. Perhaps it was an air of studied nonchalance; whatever it was, it made me realise how awkward I felt, so unsure of myself. I wanted to fit in, to feel like they felt, look like they looked, to be held in strong arms like that, and looked after.

Desperate to connect with this vibe, I almost panicked. This was exactly the kind of thing that knocked me right out of my comfort zone, and I was relieved to hear Jasmine's sweet voice whisper my name, 'Vicki,' as she naughtily beckoned me into their bedroom.

Bare-chested, unashamedly—almost brutally—masculine, Caine sat on the bed confidently, maybe even cockily, chopping up lines of coke on the mirror. He looked up as I dawdled in and laughed with pleasure. Jasmine and I responded with soft giggles as I perched next to her on the edge of the bed.

This is more my scene, I thought. *Just the three of us!* As I put my head back to appreciate the cocaine, Jasmine kissed my mouth. Soft and gentle, her lips were electrifying on mine. I savoured the moment, wondering at her femininity. So lovely to kiss another woman! To touch her soft perfumed hair, look at a face and hold a body not so different from my own! As she slithered her mouth down my neck, I felt Caine's hardness moving in. His strong arms gently grazed my slim hips to reach beyond me, to take his woman into our embrace. His strong pheromones joining her sweet scent felt indescribably beautiful. I melted into their embrace, a merging of strong muscles, trembling kisses, waves of intensity and passion that moved our bodies in a rhythmic, hypnotic ménage à trois.

A few weeks later, Jasmine said to me: 'I've got you a job, they're paying top dollar for a 'nice girl'!' Now in that context, what a 'nice girl' meant was someone who wasn't a full-time working girl, as the professionals called themselves. Sex has been for sale since time began; London during the late 1970s was no different, and whether you were buying or selling, you could take your pick. Sex workers might be happy to settle for a rich husband, perhaps an ex-punter, or preferring a little more independence they might shoot for a sugar daddy. Some were happy simply teasing for tips, as they had a 'straight' boyfriend indoors; others preferred to work on the street for speedy turnover or whatever they chose of the many variations of in between. It wasn't unusual, especially with the Arab royals, for a 'nice girl' to be requested, someone they wouldn't find on the circuit—and like the matchmakers of old who knew all the tricks of feigning virginity, those whose living depended on this trade would do their best to supply.

Astonished at the audacity of Jasmine's offer, I stared wide-eyed. What she was proposing was my first 'cherry-popping' gig.

Yes! 'I'd love to, thank you, darling!' I blurted out. I was enthralled by the idea that I would be in control: his innocence to my experience, experience just beginning to develop—*wow!*

I was starting to understand the gift of being present, sensing non-verbal cues, allowing the magic of spontaneity. The more I flowed with that energy, the easier everything became. Without ever discussing it with another soul I understood that all I had to do was tell myself to go to that place as I applied my make-up and decided what to wear. It was no different from modelling, picking up the cues from the art director and then projecting exactly the right image into the lens.

This was a huge stepping-up for a girl from a world where the theory of sex education was taught in an all-girls biology class, and the practical side was all about what boys wanted and what boys took. In London, I'd found the perfect petri dish to cultivate my girl power. Add to that the bonus of £1,000 in payment. I was thrilled, literally tickled pink! So, of all the many things whoring could be, for me, it was unquestionably a reclaiming of power.

I still had much to learn, however. In many ways, I was still a 'born yesterday' innocent, blissfully naive. I asked Jasmine, 'So how do I do it?' It was the first time I'd been in a situation where I was going to perform a definite act of sex for a definite amount of money. I wanted to know how the professionals did it. I spent hours sitting in the reception in Miss Candy's asking questions: 'Exactly at which point do I take the condom out? Should I take off my clothes first, or take a shower? Would I have to give him a blow job? How do you put the condom on? Do I make him shower? Do I just lie down, or do they expect a strip tease or something? How long do I let them carry on?' All the practical arrangements my brain needed to know so I could allow my body to go free-falling into the zone. Chuckling, the girls told me what to do; it was very clinical. I was satisfied. Now I knew the score.

Arrangements in place, off I went in a black cab to the Park Lane hotel, no fluffing my lines with the doorman this time. I looked more like a model about to meet a friend for afternoon tea than the lady of the night character I'd assumed last time. I was slimmer, more subtlety groomed, boasting an air of classiness I simply didn't possess before.

As I opened the door to the massive suite of rooms, I was instantly hit by the screeching aroma of Dior Eau Sauvage, and a base scent of mutton and Middle Eastern mezze. Not another woman in sight, not yet. *Too early for that,* I realised. I sat down and politely responded to the small talk deemed necessary—fortunately, it wasn't much. The atmosphere was of a very polite job interview, with no hint of whatever carnal thoughts may have been lurking behind their white cotton boxers purchased from Harrods.

Quietly I waited, my mind in a frenzy for something to happen.

Is my skirt too long? Am I unattractive? Where are the other bloody girls? Why is that wanker glaring at me psychopathically? Oh God!

After some confabbing in Arabic, the uncle—or the chauffeur, he was probably both—gave me the nod, took me to the next suite and pointed me to the bedroom. 'In here, is it?' I innocently asked. As diligently instructed by my friend I popped into the shower, scrubbed down, wrapped the towel around me, sauntered out and plopped the opened condom on the bedside table and sat on the bed, waiting for his knock on the door.

A minute later I heard a gentle *rap, tap, tap.*

I opened the door, and instantly the neuromotor message was transmitted at the speed of light: eyes, brain, belly, clit. *Fuck, he is hot,* I thought. He was in fact *superb.* Eyes black as coals shining from the golden skin and stately features of a royal Arabian, my mind eagerly spun: *This is going to be great; this is going to be easy, this is going to be so fucking horny!* I could see that my Arab agreed. The thobe—cool, versatile, easy to wear—left no doubt that this young man was very pleased to meet me. I gave a soft little smile of encouragement at the sight of his boner, sighing with pleasure as I lifted his thobe above his head. As I put the condom on, I kept intense eye contact, my golden Scorpio gaze into his black embers. I placed my hand on his chest in a motion that told him: *Stay there.* I had never felt as totally in control as this, ever. This beautiful specimen was all mine, and oh my I was ready: engorged, engaged and empowered!

Teasingly I stepped back, dropped my towel, and invited his eyes to gaze at my pert breasts, athletic stomach, and hairy muff. I turned around and ran my hands over my arse, spelling out its curves for him. Then slowly I bent over and put one hand on the bed and the other between my legs as I arched my back, revealing myself to him. I knew my pussy was beautiful; there were guys up and down the country wanking over it in men's magazines, so I also knew exactly what he was seeing: dark hair and bright red voluptuous lips. Provocatively tracing my manicured index finger over my swollen gland, I teased it enough to ensure my own orgasm was ready to join us. Sliding my finger easily along the glistening wet and in between those luxurious labia, my second finger followed, and I opened myself in invitation—a warm, wet, encouraging deep red cave of velvety welcoming.

I beckoned him and held the base of that fine cock so I could feel the glorious head's penetration for every single centimetre of that stretch of ecstasy, the oozing pleasure as he pushed me apart. The strength in my legs held me there as one hand worked myself and the other controlled and guided, until brute passion overtook him, and he thrust the rest of the way—in one powerful stroke he went from virginity to wildly spurting orgasm. As he exploded, a surge of energy pulsed through me, and my orgasm sucked his cock deeper inside where I clenched and gripped him. This was how a woman felt! I knew my power in that moment, and baby, I'd just earned myself a grand!

As I removed the evidence with the tissues I'd placed by the bedside, he stumbled into the shower and scrubbed himself to the seventh administrations of whatever ritual washing he adhered to—a lot, probably. I remember sitting there a long time waiting for him to appear. It wouldn't have done to leave before him.

Finally, I said my goodbyes, the same uncle paid me, and that was that. Noted in my Top Twenty Lifetime Fucks, equally graded with the big ginger farmer who lifted me up and down with his massive hands on his even more massive cock, *Last Tango in Paris*-style, until the crescendo, a seven-chakra-opening orgasm. Yes, that was on the same playing field—but as lovers went, Harry held first place … But forgive me, I am getting ahead of myself. Back then my developing sexuality and passion made my life exciting and interesting, while other elements were immensely confusing.

The seedy squats and smack I had now decided to label as home. In a sense, they were, being inhabited by people from home—the old fast-becoming-a-nostalgic-fantasy-Aberdeen—and metaphorically due to no expectations, nothing to sell, nothing to pretend, pay your money and get your fix. A place to slouch and gouch without getting your pockets picked.

St. Pauls Avenue was also home. I felt secure, but very lonely there; it was my nest. When I was modelling, I was in charge, and in control. I was a pro and I'd learnt to play the game, do the job like a pro. So long as I had a little bag to look forward to at the end of the day, all was well. People didn't pop into St. Paul's Avenue in the same way as they had on West End Lane. I'd lost Cathy and Fiona, and Curly had inadvertently become my bouncer.

Everybody from home knew him and contact with me often came that way. Truth is I would not have kept in touch otherwise. Many of the people Curly associated with were going in the wrong direction, and I started to feel a wedge growing between me and the Aberdeen I once called home.

Then someone unexpected showed me how to turn my back in style.

* * *

While the edge may have been knocked off my innocence, I still liked a good laugh and a practical joke, and my next playmates soon arrived.

Curly couldn't wait to tell me he had bumped into Sally John down in Soho: 'She looks just like a woman now!' Sally John was around our age and may have been the first gay ever to come out in Aberdeenshire. He was so famous I knew about him before I ever set eyes on him:

'Hiv ye seen 'at loon gan aboot dressed like a quine?'

'Fuck off!'

'No, 'am nae jokin', he's a bitty like David Bowie, weers make up 'n a'thing, a quine's top 'n tight jeans. He's even got his nails pintid!'

'Far dis he hing aboot.'

'Och ye'll see him gan up 'n doon Union Street.'

Sure enough, I did. Nose in the air, he minced through the centre of town. 'Quine'—Doric for female and deriving from *queen*—was the perfect word for him. Beautiful he was not. However, even in those days when it could not have been easy for a teenage boy to lay his hands on the workings of female glam, I could see Sally John had a style that could only develop with time. Already he'd managed something out of nothing. Tall, skinny, hook nose stuck in the air, make-up and a sequin boob tube, Union Street was his runway. He was also familiar with the back seat of the Wolsey.

'I'm telling you, she's classy.' Curly snapped me out of my reverie. 'She calls herself Biba.'

'"*She*"?'

'Yeah, you have to call him *she,* she's going to get a sex change.'

I was dubious, and just a little jealous. My mouth fell open when I saw Sally John for the first time. He was indeed a *she*—in fact, the kind of she I wanted to be: 'Biba'. She appeared from the basement of a nightclub off Berwick Street, strutting out like she owned the place—seething burgundy leather, high boots, blonde hair, proper tits and expensive make-up applied with the expertise of any model. The laugh on her face with the flick of the blonde hair told it all as her guttural chortle declared: 'Yes, it's me and yes, I've fucking made it!'

We all laughed; this was the stuff dreams were made of. 'Cuppa tea?'

The years flew by over several steaming mugs of strong tea and bacon butties at our favourite Soho cafe on

Broadwick Street. Eventually I met her whole gang—most, not all, at varying degrees of sex changing.

There was Hannah: tall and skinny with legs that went everywhere and often wrapped themselves around the balcony at Biba's back door, where we sat smoking and sharing the adventures of the night before, while getting ready to go out again. A dark bob a la Hepburn was her crowning grace; she proudly wore massive red pouty lips long before Botox was even a thing. Hannah was funny, cute, caustic when needed and—as is so often the case with her personality type—possessed a good helping of common sense that could smack any problems right between the eyes.

Hannah fascinated me. Every now and again she would disappear from the scene, and I'd ask Biba where she'd gotten to. 'The poor silly bitch has bouts of despair,' Biba explained. I never saw Hannah during those times. I felt extremely sad that I couldn't be there for this vivacious woman who gave me so much just by being herself.

Then there was Pearl. Pearl had been a truck driver. She was from Blackburn in Lancashire and was now a singer in the drag club under the arches in South London, another regular spot in our night-time tours. Pearl and I became close; we were both using, and she had a soft spot for me. She introduced me to Édith Piaf, and performed 'Non, Je Ne Regrette Rien' as part of her act, locking it in my heart forever.

Years later, here in my home in the Scottish Highlands, I got an unexpected call from Biba. Settled in Brighton, with a partner, a dog, and running a small successful business, she was on a rare visit up north to see her family. She broke the news that Pearl had taken her own life some years before. I played the song endlessly for the truck driver who somehow was mother, big brother and voice of my tears all rolled into one.

* * *

In those days, making a living demanded that a girl know all the options.

There were several. When there was no sugar daddy on the scene, a living could be made from prostitution on a wide boulevard in South London. I was only there once when Pearl lived nearby, so I can't remember its name; it reminded me of Bois De Boulogne.

Then there was 'clipping'. Clipping was a con whereby tourists, thinking they were buying sex, were sucked in by the tale of the cranky 'Madame' who lived upstairs. This cock-blocking wicked witch demanded payment before she'd book a room for any of the girls. Then, because of the danger of arrest, she insisted that both prostitute and punter take separate and meandering routes to arrive at said room. The clincher was the detail of the directions: they were precise and with the added precaution of exactly what to say if a policeman were to ask. This sucked the poor guy right in and off he'd go one way while we'd run off in the other direction. It was a sophisticated version of what Kiki and I had invented ourselves as we 'toured' Jersey.

I enjoyed the excitement of going out clipping with the girls. I preferred it to the seedy jobs that I did from time to time for men's magazines. This way I could hang about waiting for the good jobs to come in. In fact, I could finance not only my habit, but my growing wardrobe. High on the thrill of being able to part some unsuspecting tourist from his money, we'd laugh our way down Shaftesbury Avenue draped in our furs and jewels, acquired from the shoplifters who hung around Soho, get high on poppers, and then dance the night away. All the trannies loved my Marilyn routine, and on a night out would refer to me as Marilyn; it made us the same and I'd bring that camp glam part of my character to our nights out. There was one occasion that Biba managed to convince someone that I was a tranny too by pointing out my protruding Adam's apple—apparently a dead giveaway.

I enjoyed my nights with them. Somehow there wasn't the same ruthless competition that I experienced with heterosexual women. When my birth sisters were in London, they kind of expected that we would hang out with the models and celebs at Stringfellow's. I did it for their sake, but it wasn't for me—'Not my scene,' I explained, as it made me feel like I was arse crawling or sneaky whoring. I preferred to call things what they were.

I much preferred Biba and the gang, and usually ended up at the gay bars in the back of Covent Garden anyway. Still, there was something about living life at that level of extremity that made the downs stand out—and there were a lot of emotional ups and downs in that group.

For one, a few of us were using smack on and off. I'd been at it for two years, and it was starting to get a hold of me. I'd noticed I was 'feeling sick' more frequently. I was having to take time out of my life to hang around and score, an inconvenience that I hadn't counted on. I figured I'd take six months off, go to Australia and see if I could get clean. I was twenty-four years old, my modelling career was established, and I was certain the universe would reveal to me all of her answers.

It was time for a break.

Cathy had given me a book called *Fanny: Being the True History of the Adventures of Fanny Hackabout-Jones* before I left, and the trip turned out to be my very own version! With Candy's as a training ground, and my tranny friends as higher education, I'd learnt how to easily relieve men of large sums of money and live a life of luxury in the process.

School was out. Soon my trip Down Under would show me that I had in fact graduated first class.

CHAPTER NINE

Fanny: The Land of Plunder

It was November 1980, and David Bowie—

Ashes to ashes, funk to funky
We know Major Tom's a junkie
Strung out in heaven's high
Hitting an all-time low ...

—thumped and boomed in my head as I packed my bags.

Addiction had me strung out, like Major Tom. Addiction had become my pot of gold at the end of the rainbow. I was still some steps away from my all-time low; I didn't yet understand the true nature of the addiction beast. So it seemed to me that a world trip and six months away would naturally lead to dropping the habit. I hadn't given it any more thought than that; and besides, at Biba's suggestion I'd decided to get my boobs done. 'Plenty of us who have gone in for the change had our boobs done in Australia, darling!' she cooed. Apparently, they'd perfected the surgical technique of placing the silicone in a bag of saline solution: 'Giving the girls a more natural feel, darling'—lifting and squeezing her ample breasts to demonstrate. There was also the possibility of having the whole thing done on insurance—worst-case scenario, it would be summer. That would do, and a plan was born.

* * *

Six months! The longest I'd ever been out of the country! At twenty-four years old, it seemed like a lifetime. I organised the trip meticulously, buying a round-the-world ticket from British Airways—a wonderful deal that allowed me to stop anywhere I chose on the British Airways route and stay longer, if I fancied. Loading two large Samsonite cases with enough methadone to get me through what I imagined would be the first stage, along with three or four books, my favourite music—Pink Floyd, The Police, Dexy's Midnight Runners, some Queen and of course Led Zeppelin—and my best outfits, I chased down a cab for the airport.

For my journey, I wore an all-time favourite, the classic beige raincoat. The double-tied belt cinched my trim waist and showed off my slim calves in the 'sensible' heels I chose for travel. I'd always wanted a coat like that; eventually I'd picked it up from one of the fashion fairs in the Midlands. Never having the height to become a fashion model, I acquired some bookings at the fashion fairs on the promotional side of things. Lots of us glamour girls took these not-so-fabulously-paid jobs simply to buy the beautiful clothes offered at a discount. It was a great buy, and you can see it topped off with a trilby hat on the infamous 'Samantha Spade: Privates Detective', when I played her for a leather and rubber fashion company in the Birmingham area.

The next thing I knew I was flying from London to Rome, seated next to a guy in his early thirties on his way to a work conference. I did nothing to encourage the fellow; he asked if I had anything booked, I said no, and with a wink he replied, 'Well, you can come and crash at my hotel!' adding that his work was paying anyway. *Surprise!* The poor man was as beige as my raincoat and so predictable I almost couldn't be bothered. Still, a free hotel room was a free hotel room. *Besides, maybe it's a good idea to keep as much money as possible for my trip,* I slyly reasoned.

For the longest time, I believed that attracting this type of situation into my life was luck. My sister always used to say I could fall in the River Dee and come out with a salmon. I certainly hadn't crossed the line to looking at every interested male as a potential mark—but I had started to realise that there was more at play than Lady Luck. I just hadn't a name for it; I'm not sure that I can even name it now.

What I did know was exactly how it would play out. The instinct I'd developed during my years at Candy's gave me absolute confidence that this timid guy would cause me no trouble. *He'll be content to have a good-looking, interesting woman in the bed next to him,* I told myself—and I do mean the bed *next to him*, not next to him in the bed! The last of any doubts I had disappeared when I told the hotel reception we wanted a twin, and the fellow didn't flinch. Most men would spontaneously combust in flame, but not this chap! I slept easy, and we went out for dinner on my last night. With my first world tour bonus chalked up—free accommodation!—the trip was off to a roaring start. Checked in and boundaries clear, we jumped into our respective taxis, his taking him to work, mine for a score. My body craved that intense ripple of heroin, that comforting blast of pleasure.

This would be my last hit. Or so I told myself.

Curly had loads of Italian friends in Soho. It was hilarious when he demonstrated his mastery of the 'lingo' by gesticulating wildly with his arms and adding an 'o' to the end of English words. 'How does one say, "Fuck off, darling" in Italian?' Now I was in the centre of Rome, pumping a cab driver for the route to the nearest drug lair while making syringe-like movements on my arm. He dropped me in a beautiful historic piazza. I paid and as I turned to start hunting for a dealer, unbelievably I heard someone calling my name.

'Vicki! Bella!'

It was Sergio, an old mate from London. 'Bella, bella, *come sta?*'

Seeing the state I was in, his face turned flushed and scared. 'You sick, Bella?'

'Getting there,' I said.

'*Vieni con me.*' He smiled gently. Grabbing my arm, off we went. Two or three streets, up an alley and he pushed up my sleeve and hit me. Instantly my belly filled with light. Closing my eyes, I revelled in this blissful tide. Not bad at all.

It was not uncommon for the dealer to fix you up back then. Many people, too frightful of the needle to inject themselves, were dependent on someone else to give them a hit. I remember being frightened the first time I pulled the plunger back and watched the deep red of my blood mix with the golden liquid before pushing it into my vein, but once I learnt I was never keen to let anyone else do it for me.

Today was an exception, however; there was something about the Latin chivalry that got to me. As soon as Sergio's needle pierced the vein, I was brimming with anticipation for more. That was it then—Sergio and I were attached at the hip for the next four days. We talked and we walked. Sergio was a delightful host. He showed me every sight, from a Roman perspective. The Colosseum was approached via the backstreets, the Trevi Fountain somewhere for us to stop and take our lunch, the Basilica a place we passed on the way to a deal.

Magnifico Roma!

Next stop, Bahrain.

I was pleasantly surprised at check-in when the steward asked, 'Would you like an upgrade to first class?' *Lady Luck strikes again!* Curiously, as I boarded the plane I noticed that first class was quite empty, yet they'd seated me right next to a gentleman. *All these vacant seats, and I'm stuck with a travelling companion?* Anyway, I gave it very little thought as I was too busy enjoying the free champagne in real glasses, massive leather seats, and lots of attention from the flight staff. *This is turning out to be quite the adventure!* After they served our meal, the stewardess closed the cabin curtains, and I realised that my mysterious first-class companion and I were quite alone now.

Overcome with curiosity, I took another look.

Good-looking, Italian American, very sexy accent, broken nose, steely grey hair, tan … already I could feel the heat of his stare climbing up my neck. Dreamily I eyed his clothing. Good suit, loafers … *Quite the gangster, mmm not bad*, I thought. I was wearing a soft leather cream-coloured calf-length skirt and a pale yellow silk plunge-neckline blouse. Just the right combination of wicked and flirty.

After our dinner plates were taken away, my American gangster helped me settle in, placing the comfort blankets across both of us as if he'd known me for a hundred years. 'This all right?' he gently asked. He put his hand on my leg, gazing enquiringly as he waited for my reaction. It was one of those moments for which I will always be grateful that I took the pause. It would have been so easy to react, push his hand away, feign offence—but no, here was an opportunity for yet another adventure! *There is something about this man,* my mind trilled; handsome, suave, daring, his touch smooth and confident.

I decided not to resist. Emboldened, I looked back at him as if to inquire, *What next?* He replied by slowly tracing the outline of my knee, teasing as if he dared me to push his hand away, then with a slight ease of pressure tantalisingly moved up my inner thigh right to the point, the boundary mark. I was so relieved he stopped there—one of the tells of a good lover. It is always disappointing that so many men mistake initial permission as an invitation to jump too far, too soon. Not him—his hand caressed the underbelly of my buttocks, traced my knicker elastic before strolling down my hamstring and up my inner thigh again. Never beyond the boundary; never to the place that now begged for the touching by its sheer omission. He never did touch me there, but with perfect timing nimbly got down on his knees. Ah what a gentleman, right there in first class! I wriggled my bottom as he hitched my skirt up and pulled my panties to one side.

Hyperarousal coursed down my legs, radiating to my toes. *Don't stop. Don't stop now.* Throbbing recklessness, awake but dreaming, all my senses were on high alert. Brought back from ecstasy by the sound of the stewardess's voice as she tidied the galley behind us, the dream melted into creeping panic. Did she see? Did she hear? Had she been covering up my moans with crashing crockery? Who cared! Time to return the favour! After a few minutes of sucking him, greedy for more, I put his dick inside me, straddling him right there and then on the aeroplane seat. There it was: mile high club membership—*ka-ching!*

I never did find out who my partner in crime was, whether he'd somehow manipulated things to get me upgraded into the seat next to him. Classy all the way, he sent a bouquet to my hotel in Delhi and reserved a suite for me in Bangkok, which was our next mutual stop after Bahrain.

Bahrain was really a convenience stop along the way. In Bahrain, Abdul would be waiting. Although I referred to him as my sugar daddy, and felt glorious when he bestowed gifts upon me, the truth is I'd grown to love Abdul over time. He had an endearing childlike quality about him, we had lots of laughs—and so I was very sad when I didn't see his chubby face and big grin waiting for me at Bahrain airport.

Martin, Abdul's 'other friend', arrived to meet and greet me instead. Abdul couldn't get to Bahrain on that occasion, I was told. I'd have full use of his apartment, of course, conveniently next door to Martin's. And being Abdul, he'd left me a tidy wad to continue my journey.

Originally I'd met Martin at Abdul's home in Abu Dhabi. His beautiful villa was surrounded by a towering wall, with grazing goats in the garden, sadly slaves who slept on the kitchen floor, and a sitting room big enough for a hundred people. The bedrooms were in the basement, and as was trendy at the time the beds and furniture were suede: Abdul's brown, Martin's blue, and mine the most horrendous salmon pink. The colour coding didn't stop there. A whole back wall of his yard was full of cars, Cadillacs in every shade you can imagine.

I don't think I'd realised just how rich Abdul must have been until I saw that. When Abdul went out for business for the day, Martin and I had our choice of chariot. My favourite was the mint-green convertible. There were also Mercedes, Rolls Royces, Lamborghinis, Ferraris. Fortunately, Martin was great company. We'd zoom along the new highways being built, admiring the gleaming glass skyscrapers going up—what a transformation! Often, we'd go shopping in the souk, never with less than a grand each to spend. Abdul doled out cash in the morning before he vanished to work—our pocket money for the day, so we'd cruise around gossiping about what we'd do with all the money we planned to make, and the life we'd enjoy when we retired.

In Bahrain I met Martin's partner, Jim, a beautiful man with Paul Newman eyes and short-cropped white-blonde hair. We caught up, had a few laughs, I sipped my methadone and rested up before the next leg of the journey. Both Martin and Jim worked for an airline, and being that I was about to venture further East than I ever had in my life, I asked their advice about how safe it would be for me travelling alone.

Martin was reassuring: 'Tell people you work for British Airways, Vicki. Then they will understand that someone is looking out for you. And you never know, you might even get a discount at the hotels.' That piqued my interest, we talked a little more about that strategy and off I went … Delhi, here I come!

* * *

My next flight companion was a forty-four-year-old Venezuelan woman. Independent-minded and feminist, she had her own travel agency and boasted that she had a younger live-in lover, whom she happily left behind to enjoy the perks of being in the travel business. I was full of admiration—but then she pushed me into the competition zone by bragging about the 15 percent discount she'd receive at her Delhi hotel. *Seriously, did you just raise the gauntlet, bitch?*

On arrival in Delhi, I was awestruck. Firstly, by the sheer surging masses of people packed in the airport as we queued like sardines to squeeze out of the place. A young boy persistently tugged at my clothes—'Take your case, lady? Yes? No?'—others joined in vying for my attention as I struggled in my 'sensible heels' to the exit: 'Car this way, ma'am!' 'Taxi outside, come with me, miss!'

Eventually I thrust my way into a cab. 'Sheraton!' I ordered. This decision was made in a flurry, partly due to the 'competition' with the travel agent, partly because of Martin's suggestion. The clincher was that the Delhi sights and sounds were so overwhelming, I simply needed that cool marble facade to drain away the pulsating panic in my brain.

The city was a lot to take in. So many people! So many colours! Five-lane traffic with everything from the sacred cow, pushbikes, rickshaws, tumbledown jalopies, and smoke-belching trucks. Let's not forget the good old Ambassador car. I'd never experienced such a cacophony of colour, sights, smells, and sounds in one place. I can still see it in my mind; it's what drew me back all these years later. I recall the feeling that hit my gut when I saw the family living in the ditch at the bottom of the drive to the Sheraton. It tolled like a bell in my head—*wrong, wrong, wrong*!—accompanied by the sickening realisation of just how evil humankind can be. *Me too,* I thought. I was one of the bad ones, driving up to my five-star bed. That was confusing.

Martin had been right about hotel staff easily accepting that I was flight crew. Although I was nervous, the receptionist simply asked, 'Which airline?' to which I blurted out, 'British Airways!'—but oops, then he asked to see my ID. I fumbled in my bag: 'Oh so sorry, erm, I must have left it in my luggage …,' trying hard to sound posh. Meanwhile I felt my heart rate climbing, sweat beading on my hands, my arms, everywhere. 'No problem, ma'am, just bring it down with you next time.' The reception clerk smiled, handing me my room key.

Mouth dry, muscles clenched, brain still locked in raw fear, I snatched the key. Fifty percent discount, *boom!*

The hotel bed was plush and comfortable. I woke after a fourteen-hour sleep feeling sick enough not to want to make the journey to Agra. Not without a score, anyway. I'd been asking around and it wasn't a particularly easy trip. Mentally I calculated: I was going to spend two days in India, two days in Bangkok, and two in Singapore. I had no idea how I would take to these places. I had the option that if I fell in love with any of them, I could always stay on. I'd also considered going to Chiang Mai; I'd met other travellers who had been there. Back in London it had crossed my mind that if I visited Chiang Mai, I might never come back. Here in my Delhi bedroom, I crossed that possibility off my list forever.

Coming down off smack, my nervous system felt jagged. My hands were clammy, and I was more than a little wobbly inside. Perhaps I hadn't properly considered what coming off would feel like; maybe I hadn't been without heroin that long before or maybe the times when I was, I had been distracted by something else. I realised this was the first time heroin officially stopped me from doing something that I wanted to do. Agra would have to wait.

I jumped in a rickshaw and said, 'Take me to the European campsite.' The driver nodded, having no problem with that. And I sat in the back bombing through the streets of Delhi with the warm breeze blowing my hair, beginning to feel half human again, I promised myself one thing.

That I would come back.

At the European campsite, I staggered out of the rickshaw. 'Where's the guys from Aberdeen?' I asked. The campsite was much bigger than I'd imagined; finding them took several more enquiries along the way. Scoring wasn't that straightforward either. Another rickshaw ride later, we ended up in a carpet shop where the owner and his brother—a fact that they seemed overly keen to ensure I understood—were more interested in making an export deal where I would buy carpets and they would hide heroin inside them. He gave us what we wanted in the end, but the smack was flavoured; it must have been cut with something. Whatever it was, it reminded me of the Emporium, a shop at the bottom of Castle Street in

Aberdeen that stocked knick-knacks from all over the world that set my childish imagination on fire.

Anyway, that was Delhi, little more than a flavoured score and room service. Fuck, what was happening?

I toted enough with me to Bangkok to take the edge off, just a little bit to snort. I didn't dare carry works; instead, I carried a sadness with me that hung around the rest of that trip and beyond. I was so disappointed that I miscalculated the length of time it would take me to get to Agra, and confused as to why I hadn't even thought that out. But seeing the European campsite and the ease with which I scored the heroin, I knew that staying on wasn't a great idea either. I decided to worry about it all when I got to Sydney.

This was my emotional state when I arrived in Bangkok. I didn't fall in love with it at all. Bangkok was busy, noisy, dirty and smelly. I flew in with my friend from Venezuela and as we sat on the plane, she recounted stories of her time in India, of the little girl in the family-run hotel where she stayed who kept knocking at her door with 'gifts': little bottles of water. One day the little girl left her a sandwich; later my friend was horrified to discover it was monkey! I wondered if it was true, or if something had gotten lost in the translation; either way I was grateful not to have experienced anything like that. However, listening to all the places she'd visited in a mere two days, I felt a pang of regret and wondered, *What am I doing with my life?*

This time we shared a cab from the airport. I went to check out a couple of hotels with her along the way. One had a rat in the corridor; no way I was staying anywhere like that, so once again I opted for the Sheraton. It was even nicer than the one in Delhi. This was my second time playing air hostess and I must have raised my game because the receptionist simply asked, 'British Airways?'

'Yes, thank you, darling!'

I didn't call Mr Mile High at his hotel as promised though. The truth was I knew something about myself by the time I reached Bangkok—something I hadn't been aware of when I stepped into first class in Rome, and I didn't want to face that through the eyes of someone else. Instead, I slunk into the luxurious Sheraton bathrobe and plucked up the phone. 'Book me a massage, please?'

It was quite wonderful, and unlike any massage I'd experienced before. I guess it was a Thai massage. The masseuse used pressure points particularly around my pelvic region. I caught my breath when out of nowhere my body spontaneously orgasmed as she pushed my folded knee beyond the other leg into a full-body twist. I spent a lot of time thinking about how that had happened; was it the mysterious skills of the East? Although I was topping up with a bit of smack here and a little methadone there, my body was in withdrawal from the numbness I'd been plying it with since my return from Chicago almost three years prior. Thrust into hyperreality, I yearned to be alone with my thoughts. I had a swim washing some of those thoughts away, then sat by the pool in my robe and plucked up the phone again. 'Room service?'

I'd done lots of solo travelling by then, and enjoyed dinner in the company of a good novel. The book, the surroundings and the food were all good. The room was otherwise empty, so of course I noticed the Arab gentleman and his lackey sitting a couple of tables back. His eyes had been eating me for dessert as I swam up and down the pool. There was no need for me to look around or communicate with them; I knew he was staring; I could feel the psychic heat and intensity of it. I didn't have the energy to even think about it but when I asked for my cheque, the waiter nodded in the Arab's direction and said, 'That's been taken care of, ma'am.' Bloody hell! Here we go again, another fool and his money thinking he could buy everything.

The Arab gentleman appeared again at breakfast, asked me to join him, and share the day shopping. There was nothing better to do. Silks, jade, tailor-made clothes to order, all the things I'd planned on anyway with Muhammad footing the bill … perhaps I'd go round the world and even make a profit at this rate. Poor man got a hard-on in the silk shop, and I realised this was no well-hung Abdul. However, he managed to contain himself and the day went well.

Dinner at the hotel that evening was a semi-pleasant struggle with his twenty words of English, and my twenty words of Arabic. Still, I owed him that much. Only ten minutes after we said goodnight, I heard his fists pounding at my door. *Bang, bang, bang!* 'Oh fuck off!' I bellowed. I called security and that was that.

Next day I flew to Singapore. He phoned me that night at the hotel and told me he was coming to Singapore after me. I refused to see him in Singapore, though we met for coffee when he came to London the following year. Choosing Knightsbridge for our rendezvous, I was secretly hoping for another shopping spree. That didn't happen; neither did anything else. I wasn't looking for a long list of sugar daddies. When I found myself in those situations, I simply went with the flow, *if* it amused me. I was okay about taking money from the men at Candy's and I liked Abdul. Somehow this would have been different, and I just wasn't up for it. *I don't need his dirty oil money,* I reasoned. Stop plundering the earth—what was wrong with people? Greedy bastards!

Singapore was a flash-in-the-pan, high-rise buildings full of shops. I bought a £10 bag of shitty smack on the street and shared my hotel room with a South African pilot I met in the airport. When I boarded the Qantas jet to Sydney I was on a downer. The only bonus there was getting the whole three seats to myself, where I could pop a pill and get some sleep. Imagine my horror when the giant, dirty blonde, bad-skinned, crass-mouthed Aussie steward kneed me in the feet to wake and warn me, 'Fasten your seatbelt, we're about to land.' *Ewww!* That first interaction just about sums up my whole time in Australia: the land Down Under was more like the Land of Plunder, hold on to your soul. Even the smack was crap. White stuff I guess they shipped from Thailand, it just didn't hit the spot, and was nothing compared to the brown sugar I was used to. *Oh shit, I'm going to have to tough this out,* I told myself, faking a smile to hide my grinding depression.

My mother's uncle picked me up at the airport and took me to their house south of Sydney. The beaches were incredible, and having to put on a brave face for family helped me through those uncomfortable few days. I got to know my grandfather's younger brother who had been demobbed in Australia after the Second World War. He showed me around, took me prawning, allowing me to dry out a little bit, and I didn't feel too bad by the time he dropped me off in the Bondi Beach bedsit I'd managed to rent. Bondi was one of those places you always thought would be on your must-see list if you ever visited Australia. I hadn't realised it was a junkie and crime paradise. I was burgled three times in that bedsit. The burglaries only ceased because I had nothing else for them to pinch. All the things that I bought from my journey—the beautiful jade and the silk pillowcases I'd bought my mother—all gone.

Were there some good moments? A few. I did some PR work, crazy stuff like sitting in the middle of Sydney with a Kodak cardboard box over me giving out leaflets. I investigated the beautiful city of Sydney, got an agent and one job as Marilyn. However, I got nowhere at all with the couple of movie castings I attended. I befriended a girl who lived nearby; she introduced me to a strip club in Kings Cross. There I did one or two shifts, but this was no Miss Candy's. It was such a filthy dive—coarse, like back in the days of the gold rush. Australia was a strange mixture of that, extreme coarseness on the one hand and unsubstantiated snobbery and racism on the other. I'd expected a Disneyesque magical kingdom; in shock I found a ghostly country purged of magic. So, I never settled.

My Bondi Beach friend was also a user. Lucky me. I did use while I was there, but somehow the Aussie smack never really got quite the same hold on me. Through a friend of a friend, I did get my tits done on the insurance of someone's ex-wife, performed by the surgeon all the trannies went to. My tan was amazing and so was my hair, now sun-bleached to a beautiful blonde. I enjoyed spending most of my life in a bikini and a loose kaftan. However, I got the shock of my life when I dressed for my flight to Hawaii—none of my clothes fit, even my shoes didn't want to go on my feet. How did I get so bloated and swollen? I had gained weight and had no idea why. I was an unhappy woman when I sat on that plane, and I still had no idea what I was going to do with the rest of my life.

I slept for two days in Hawaii, no denying what that was all about, swallowing pills to tide me over, lying on the beach in a sweat-soaked sarong. I met up with Gina, my modelling pal from London in LA. She brought me some methadone, it got me through, and we stayed for three weeks with Cathy's Dale, who was now acting, went to a couple of kinky Hollywood parties, a fab outdoor disco—we ticked the boxes. Las Vegas, San Francisco, and New York. I'd never had a yearning for America, even Hollywood; it was simply a sightseeing trip. We enjoyed it well enough, I lost some of the weight along the way, but I knew I was marking time. I didn't speak about it, I didn't even think about it, but deep inside I knew that six months had gone by, and I'd failed to kick the habit. I just wanted to get home.

CHAPTER TEN

The Peep Show: Lock, Stock and Throbbing Barrel

Determined to spin my life back on an upswing, I took the plunge. I purchased a four-bedroom garden flat in Cavendish Road, Kilburn.

It was 1982. A new conversion of a large Victorian house, the kitchen opened into an airy lounge with large windows and French doors gazing out to the back garden, patio, lawn, and off-road parking. The open fire had a brickwork chimney with bookshelves and stereo system on either side of it; the opposite wall—also open brickwork—sported a leopard-skin rug, a gift from an admirer. Beautiful Italian cream leather sofas sat around a pale beech coffee table, and soft peach-coloured silk drapes hung next to venetian blinds of deeper autumnal shades. There were two fully tiled bathrooms, and my bedroom backed on to the street with the essential bay window.

I adored every inch of it.

I had an Equity card now. This meant better agents, work in films, walk-on parts and small roles for BBC: *Cannon and Ball, EastEnders,* and more. I was proud to be directed by Cubby Broccoli while shooting the title sequence in *Moonraker* and honoured to work on a sketch with the great comedy duo The Two Ronnies. Loads of lookalike gigs as Marilyn were also coming my way. There were flights to Hamburg, Frankfurt, Amsterdam, Paris. I was greeted at the airport with flowers, stared at in shopping malls, and signed autographs as people crowded in line whispering Miss Monroe's name. My interpretation of Marilyn was so easy; even the lateness was in character, the make-up and ruby-red pouting lips hiding the trembling junky inside.

* * *

She arched her back over the sensuously smooth red satin, extending her arm overhead in an open invitation as impatient fingers played along the curve of that heart-shaped bed. Breasts taut, nipples soft and warm, head thrown back, eyelids heavy with anticipated ecstasy. Lips full, red, open, breathless. Her pupils dilated at the sight of her lover:
'Nescoré' she whispered ...

'Cut! Christ! Make-up!'

In dismay the assistant director sighed, turning to the make-up artist in disgust. The lights had melted my Leichner Camera Clear stage foundation, revealing the blue thrombosis sloping towards the red volcanic soul scar on my arm. Veins that had once been as voluptuous as my lips, as smooth as the satin I'd lain on, were now covered in jagged souvenirs.

Scurrying to the cold toilet, I slapped my arm hard to make a vein rise. The needle nipped as I forced it to tear flesh. *I bloody hate fixing in the cold*, I thought, as I shivered my way back to Ken Russell and his glass walking stick.

During that Nescoré commercial, shot at Wembley Studios, I was spotted for the lead next to Sting in *Quadrophenia*. Several call-backs later, they chose someone else. *Fuck me.* Now I was at a teeter point: life could go either way, the stakes had just gotten higher, my habit along with it. I was using regularly and using a lot. I had my own Persian dealer now, Toni. Toni's father had worked for the Shah of Iran, he was educated, discreet and always brought the very best of brown. I rarely suffered a dry spell. Toni was always there for me, we were friends. Along with a couple of others from my inner circle, we had takeaway and videos delivered, then sat around gouching.

That was exactly how I wanted it.

* * *

After the film shoot, I slouched back home to Cavendish Road. Having such a beautiful home attracted its share of visitors. At one point, both of my sisters, my six-year-old niece, Sarah, and my sister Kim's boyfriend, were all living there.

Every morning, dear old Mr Everett—'the butler', as my sisters called him—would show, just as he probably had done his whole working life. He'd set the faded stripey fold-up chair he brought with him (my sofas were too low for him) in his special spot, where he could see all the toings and froings of the household. Phone at the ready on a table, next to his roll-ups, so he could answer without getting up, Mr Everett coughed and spluttered into the handset: 'Miss Scott's residence?' Mr E was cool. Eccentrically, he always wore at least two or three wristwatches, one that ran a little fast and the other a little slow. He needed to be sure of the exact time, and as futile as it was, he was always on my case trying to encourage punctuality when I was working.

'When are you going to get rid of that smelly old bastard?' my youngest sister Lisa asked. That question rattled me. 'Mind your own, you spoiled little shit!' I spat back. Lisa could be like that. I often felt she was pretentious, arrogant, spoilt, and lacking compassion.

I remember when she came with Mum to West End Lane. She could have only been about twelve years old. I can still see her seated on Cathy's bed, wearing the sulkiest of countenances. *What now?* my mind sighed. She was Mum's youngest, and since Mum and Dad were making a little bit of money now, they enjoyed spoiling her. I got a little of that too, but in a different way. I had Mum and Dad all to myself during my early years and received their undivided attention. It was money that was in short supply back then. I was grateful for that, as it gave me an ability to be hungry, to go out in the world and make it for myself.

Mum, obviously feeling uncomfortable, told Cathy and me that Lisa didn't want to stay the night. 'We're going to a bed and breakfast, round the corner,' she declared. What a kick in the teeth! West End Lane was no palace, but it was clean—plus, Cathy and I had put in a huge effort for the visit. I saw the way Cathy looked at me; her stone-cold silence said it all.

I knew Mum would never have made that suggestion of her own accord. Mum had been brought up poor; she told me she knew what hunger felt like, recalling how tight things were during the war when Grandad was away in Africa. She remembered going to the chipper and starving, ripping through the newspaper, and gobbling down handfuls of the chips on the road home despite knowing it meant a sharp 'clap 'round the lug' when she got there. Sleeping five in a bed—that was the norm in Mum's day. Another was keeping the shopkeeper busy weighing the tatties in the back shop while Grandma put a few extra cans in her shopping bag.

Cathy understood: her folk were like that, too—couthy and caring, not a stuck-up bone in their body. So even back then when she was so young, I felt like my sister radiated petty poison towards me. I had no idea why—*Was it jealousy? Did she covet my glamorous life?* Whatever it was, that was the first but certainly not the last time I smelt its foul breath. So, I was surprised when all these years later she told me she was coming to London.

* * *

I knew Kim would be there. Kim had always loved me, looked up to me. She had even run away when she was twelve with her best friend, Maggie, to come and live with me. But Lisa—that acidic princess puzzled me. Still, I was willing to try; she was my sister despite the rift between us. In that moment though I was hurt by her snide remarks about Mr E, incensed at her hard heart and inability to see that being needed gave an old man a bit of life. Mr E had in fact dedicated himself to me; he was loyal and kind and looked after me in every little way that he could.

Then there was Olga the cleaner. Olga was my stalwart; she'd been with me from the start of Kilburn and stayed until the day, both of us broken, I was forced to walk away. We grew close over those years and shared many of our life's ups and downs. She and Mr E were my protectors.

As for my trusty steed—well, that sat unused in the car park since my successive driving bans, which annoyingly were less about my driving and more about the local cops knowing me. They loved to take me down to the local nick, lock me in a cell and then charge me with anything from baldie tyres to no insurance, while in the meantime giggling like stupid schoolboys as they took turns peeking through the peephole at the Page 3 girl in the cell. Having lost the power to pilot my own vehicle was bloody inconvenient, so for a while I had to have a chauffeur, too.

I also had a personal knicker washer who turned up every week and paid me to handwash the household smalls—well, mine anyway. That was the first of many rows over money with my sisters:

'The knicker washer's coming today, put your dirty drawers in there.'

'How much?'

'How much, fuck you, ye greedy little bastard! You'll get a cut when you start paying your way!'

'Well, that pervert's not getting to wash mine unless I get something!'

'You can fuck right off and wash your own smelly knickers then, ye tappin' cunt!'

It was always like that. I blamed Mum and Dad for spoiling them; I felt that they were so entitled and demanding, and I didn't appreciate the vibe it created in my lovely new home.

I did love that my young niece was there, and really enjoyed spoiling her when I got the chance. Kim did clean and put a meal on the table, so she wasn't so bad; but generally, they were lazy, thinking they were on the gravy train. Like Dad said many years later, annoyed with them for not confessing I was in trouble: 'Milkin' i bloody coo!'

They had no idea the hard yards I put in to get where I was. They complained when I had my junky friends around, warned me that Olga and Mr E were using me. Classic projection! Neither of them had ever paid me a penny rent, and even complained if I asked them to help clear up: 'Get yer fuckin' slaves to do it!' If I offered them a job, they'd accuse me of trying to put them on the game; and if I ever asked them to contribute, they'd question my ability to keep it together and wonder out loud if Mum and Dad should know I was using. 'It would kill Ma if she ever found out the state you were in! Maybe you need their help though …' When Kim's boyfriend started using too; things got tougher all around. I felt hurt and used. Free digs for family had a shelf life, for sure.

This was the price I paid in exchange for the success story of the young Scottish lass gone south. It wasn't the only one.

On the one time when both Mum and Dad came to visit, I got Jerry the limo driver to pick them up at the airport and be at their service with his beautiful white Mercedes. It was a special treat, one that was a joy to give—but in doing so I placed myself in a position where I was seen as 'Mr Big', a role that was hard to cast off later.

Eventually the psychic torment and angst got the best of me. I was sick of my sisters poncing off me on one hand and complaining about the dark side of what I did on the other. They especially hated it when I'd get stoned and give things away. 'What, you gave that new handbag to a junky?' 'Your fox fur to that twat, I would have had that!' I was a work machine, pursuing an acting career and maintaining an ever-increasing drug habit. There were times when ends didn't quite meet, yet others when it seemed I was a cash magnet. My sisters wanted a share of one and none of the other.

Speaking of cash magnet brings me back to Abdul. Our friendship had started to crumble. I was using him as my personal ATM, and he saw through it. By then there were other Arabs; one night on a date with the guy whose personal game of Monopoly had just acquired him the best of Park Lane, I won ten big ones at the casino. I had never seen so much money in my life! When I returned home in the early hours of the morning, I spread the notes end to end throughout the flat. I felt like fucking Ivana Trump!

Another time, I was given a ten grand 'gift' from a member of the Saudi security team; basically, a fuck-off fee to leave the Carlton Hotel in Cannes quietly when a miscommunication on the contract occurred. Not that I would have said anything out loud in the lobby if things had gone that way. It turned out to be a great trip: I slummed it two or three hotels down the esplanade, had my hair done in braids a la Demi Moore, fell in with a young Jewish New Yorker I met on the beach while she was having panic attacks—apparently the Arabs were straight out trying to haggle for a night with her right there on the sand. We hired a car and drove to the Italian Riviera. When it wasn't hot enough for our liking, we flew to Casablanca for a 'rest' before heading back to our respective homes.

One of the UK's top nude models for several years now, having proved popular with the readership, I eventually went all-in with the men's mags. I had my own column: *The Diary of Vicki Scott* and enjoyed making up the larger-than-life stories that were quite preposterous yet taken in, lock, stock, and throbbing barrel. It wasn't huge money, but it was regular. I knew my career had a sell-by date and I wanted the best chance of being able to retire. I also had a habit to consider, so when one of the East End boys from Soho approached me explaining they were stepping back to landlord status and offering trusted friends the tenancy, it was a no-brainer. The Soho comeback: *Vicki Scott's Peepshow and Fantasy Studios.* I was the first woman in Soho to open her own peep show, and the first owner to ever dance in her own establishment.

Soho had always been a cacophony of characters. Simply walking from the sandwich bar to the studio was a floor show of life unseen elsewhere. Ian Drury's studios were across the road; he and I often stopped to enjoy a chinwag when passing on the street. There were lots of casting agencies with size-8 fashion models hovering about. Then there were the studios, like the one where I'd shot the video for XTC's hit 'Are You Receiving Me?' You might even spot a soap star grabbing an Indian with a real-life Soho gangster. Then there were the club staff, the heavies, the strippers, the trannies and the street girls and boys. Let's not forget the 'tea leaves'—West End's shoplifters, cut-price suppliers of all designer wares. And of course, those who made all the wheels turn: the punters.

The huge black and red doors that screamed *Vicki Scott's Peepshow* opened into an innocuous sex shop with a counter on the left, three or four porn booths on the right, and six kiosks straight ahead: *The Peep Show Palace!* The punters walked straight in to find themselves facing a mechanical letter box with a £1 coin slot. They'd insert the coin to make the box open, revealing one or two semi-naked dancers on a raised stage. It was a modern-day version of Miss Candy's, where the punter could squeeze tips through a gap in the letter box to entice the girl to come closer and gyrate on his glass. All he had to do was keep the coins coming: *clink, clunk, ka-chunk!* The satisfying sound of coins dropping on coins through the slot into plastic pails in the locked cupboard below became more muffled as the pails filled up, and if the peepshow was a sitcom, emptying time had to be top of the bill.

My partner Boff—a young boxer with cauliflower lugs, a broken nose, and bandy legs—hailed from the Edgeware Road. Whenever the coffers were full, we'd tell the girls to grab a cuppa, call in reinforcements, close the doors, then drag the overflowing yellow buckets out of their locked cupboards. Three of us would run up Berwick Street lugging two buckets apiece to Boff's other, quieter shop to count it. During the mad dash, we'd pocket as much for ourselves as we could without the other seeing. Boff was faster than me, teetering on my stilettos, and always managed to get in behind his till and put a smile of feigned innocence on his face before I got there. Bloody thug!

Boff ran the shop; the peep show was fifty-fifty between us, and I took the rental for the two modelling studios at the back of the house. I provided the girls, Boff the security. Boff and I were around the same age; he had a wife and kids well away from our place of business. Then there were the girls, each with their own heartbreaking story. Just like in Candy's, some were passing through as they ran from their own demons, others like me seeking fame and fortune. There was never a dull moment. Even our cleaner—fuck yes, someone *had* to do it—had his own little side hustle.

Mannie the mop was literally hung like a donkey—a weighty tool, long, thick, brown, and beautiful, a sight many punters were willing to pay handsomely to feast their eyes upon. For us, it was just another day at the office, albeit a colourful and interesting one—much like the day Donald, Boff's front door man, rushed through the back and hissed:

'Hide, for fuck's sake!'

He didn't need to ask twice. I left my half-finished coffee on the desk, pushed past the curtain into the peep show, signalled the girls to cover the flaps for a sec, stood on the shelf that housed the money pails and pulled myself up into the dead space above the peep show mechanics and stayed there cowering.

When Donald came back, stretching his arms up to help me down—'You're alright, babe, I got rid of 'em'—all I could do was laugh. He was a big guy with one of the most placid personalities I knew. To see him so rattled, almost in tears, coupled with the relief of getting out of hiding, just about ended me. Apparently, some South London gangsters had come calling with their sawn-off shotguns looking for Boff. Donald wasn't taking the chance that I might do instead.

Then there was the press coverage after radical feminists threw a brick through our window. That puzzled me—what happened to Germaine Greer's self-determination? Us girls were independent and doing alright for ourselves. I never thought past that; none of us did, it was our choice, *wasn't it?*

Much as there was loads to love about the peep show—new perversions to discover daily, plenty of laughs—I hated having to go in every day to protect my cut. Everyone had their fingers in the pie, and it was a chore policing it. Punters who'd seen me in the mags travelled far and wide to get a glimpse, but I started to avoid dancing in the booth. I was tired, jaded, and yes, I was getting tough. I'd finally accepted I was a junky. And although I never completely forgot the nameless yet ever-present hurt deep inside, I'd come to accept it was part of me, something I'd never work out. I spent more and more time just gouching out; work was becoming an annoying interference. Even the glittering parts—party invites, eating and drinking in London's top spots, paid holidays—none of it ticked the box anymore. I'd attend if it was extra special or I felt I had to career-wise, or when I was in a 'pretending to be normal' phase.

That's where I was at when I met Terry.

* * *

'No, no, sex isn't expected,' my agent waffled on as I padded about the kitchen, in my PJs and fluffy slippers. 'You just have to sweeten 'em up, some important business deal. Wear something classy, look at 'em like they're the best thing since sliced bread, and make sure they have a great time, you know the score.' Sticking the kettle on, I was already mentally dressing: Nina Ricci cream silk blouse, super-soft pale yellow leather skirt, and yes, I can wear those new heels, soft muted lipstick, just a little gloss. My agent agreed to let me round up the other girls—great, that was always a boost for the favour jar.

Sharing cheek-to-cheek kisses and quick girly catch ups, the four of us gathered in the lobby before getting into the elevator to the penthouse. It was a new hotel, offering a stupendous view of Knightsbridge from the penthouse lounge where we met our hosts: typical Arab dignitaries and unusually, two Americans. I was instantly drawn to Terry, who—at six foot two with blue eyes and arms as thick as an average guy's thighs—I guessed played American football. It was clear that he was the one making the deal; the fact that his mate merged into the background quietly and everyone else was wearing a thobe or a skirt was a dead giveaway.

The Saudis spent the evening speaking to each other in Arabic, none of them apparently interested in us girls. Apart from my curiosity about Terry and what they were up to, it was quite boring. I was relieved when it wrapped up early and delighted to be invited along with one of the other girls, Micky, for drinks at the quiet guy's South Kensington flat.

'Come on, let's get you girls a drink! The night's still young!'

A little small talk and a few polite sips later, Terry took the glass from my hand and lifted me up so he could look straight into my eyes. It was the most natural thing in the world to wrap my arms and legs around him as he carried me to the bedroom. We collapsed on the bed, laughing. I had never any doubt that I'd end up in bed with him—he was lovely, full of passionate kisses and lovemaking that was both gentle and sincere. It wasn't long before I was on that beautiful plateau of bliss enjoying every minuscule movement, feeling my body respond to his. Sensing into it, he turned us over, and as I straddled him, he placed his hands around my waist, literally taking my full weight as I moved on him. Then he took charge, guiding me to a new pleasure. My body let go to the rhythm of his strong and steady beat and my orgasm crashed around me like a thundering wave. He joined the thrusting momentum, raising us higher than seemed possible, merging us deeper into the shuddering crescendo of bliss. *Wow, not bad for a first time!* With a heroin habit, an orgasm took a bit of know-how; you can take my word for that. Thus, Terry earned his place in my Hall of Fame, and I was smitten.

I loved that he called later that same day: 'There's a cute little bistro near my apartment, let's have dinner tomorrow night.' In a Knightsbridge basement, it was in fact one of London's chicest; an expensive celebrity hot spot. Sharing snippets of our lives during our getting-to-know-you conversation, Terry told me he was from New York. 'An arms dealer,' he confessed without blinking an eye. Our evening passed easily, with laughter and good food. We strolled back to his flat holding hands and after making love on his ultra-comfortable bed I fell into a deep sleep.

Somewhere in the darkness, as I slumbered, my brain began bristling with evil little memories. When I woke inside the immaculate bachelor apartment, with its tiny balcony overlooking rooftops straight out of the *Mary Poppins* movie, every single personal demon I'd ever had came rushing back to haunt me.

I sat up, swaying. The fact that I'd been lying in this gorgeous man's arms after an evening of intimate talk and passionate lovemaking made absolutely no difference. *Stop it!* I told myself, as the love feeling started to cascade over me. *You're kidding yourself. He'll never go for you, just look at this place! A guy with sheets like that is never going to love someone like you—untidy, lazy, clumsy, can't even do your own cleaning, slut!* 'He probably has a cleaner in every day,' I argued back with myself. *Big deal! He probably has some superpowered sorority girl back home cooking him turkey for Thanksgiving as well. You, you're just a novelty, a cute little notch on his belt, his British model friend!*

The words rattling in my brain hurt. I was so self-critical; my inner bitch knew no bounds when she turned on me. I had neither the awareness nor the language to realise I was reliving memories of Chicago and hurts from way before then. Memories of a little girl standing alone under the laburnum tree—

'Snelling is smelling in the middle of the spelling! Snelling is smelling in the middle of the spelling!'

Retreating from those voices, I curled up inside myself. Cold and withdrawn, I made some excuse to Terry—'Must get ready for a modelling job … Bye!'—and rushed home to the comfort of my untidy bed and my friend, the needle.

Miraculously, Terry came back for more. I guessed I had the supporting role in his London story: pubbing on the King's Road, drives into the country, roast beef at the Carlton Rooms for Sunday lunch. About four dates later, one night as we lay in bed, Terry told me about a deal he was hoping to pull off in Dubai. 'Would you fly over to sweeten the deal for me, baby? Might be fun—a bit of socialising, holiday feel, you can take Micky with you if you like. I'll give you ten grand on departure and another ten on completion.'

For a moment I lay there, trying to make sense of it all. Then my doubts melted. Like I was going to say no to ten grand up front!

'Sure,' I managed to squeak out.

Of all the things that I could have worried about in a situation like that, my deepest worry was his feelings for me. *What if the situation transpired that the best thing to do was to sleep with the client? What then? Would Terry care?* I ridiculed myself; I'd slept with this guy half a dozen times; I wouldn't have dared ask him how he felt about me. I met him through business, he just wanted me to seal the deal. In fact, all these dinners and intimate dates were probably about him working out if I would be savvy enough to carry it through. *He probably isn't an arms dealer at all! Just some arms dealer's pimp, sent to prime up girls to close deals with the fuckin' Saudis!* I didn't understand why they needed to do that at all, though; it didn't add up. Terry'd approached me through my agent, I only had his Knightsbridge number, and I only knew what he told me …

Micky's doubts went even deeper: 'We'll end up in a brothel or some kind of harem!' she pleaded in a panic.

'Don't be stupid!' I countered. 'Look, whatever it is, it's not *that*. And anyway, I already have the first ten grand, so we're going!'

Micky needn't have worried. We were refused entry at the border due to the Israeli stamp on my passport—another half-hearted attempt to dry out earlier that year. That was that. That was Terry. He could go back to his sorority girl, ironed sheets, and bigoted waspish life. Who did he even think he was? He couldn't have me anyway.

CHAPTER ELEVEN

Methadone Dreams and Magpies

I am the Queen
Dancing to the sitar
Adorned in gaudy gems
Bathed in amber's deepest musk.

Brown eyes agonisingly adoring.
Rushing my blood and moving my hips
To a fierier and fiercer vibrating rhythm
To a promise of encasing rapture, the sweet delight of
honeyed fountains,
And blissful sleep.

I wasn't sure if I'd come or not. Did he notice? Nah, he didn't, eyes fixed on the road. Copper. I'd been thinking of that time in Bahrain—the tent, the road, that fear. The star-filled night, desert cold and the sweet delicacies at the table. I must have nodded.

Exotic encounters I'd never take home,
Forbidden love, bought and sold,
But no less enjoyed.
Within the bargain,

The freedom of releasing the body
To pleasures yet unknown
In more familiar terms.

And yet here I was, driving over Glen Shee, waking from my methadone dream. Beside me sits Nick, blue eyes, blonde hair: 'Nick, Nick, the double-barrelled dick' as Cathy called him. I must stop sharing my intimate details with her—yes, he had been gifted in the girth department, and I suppose I had used the words 'double-barrelled shotgun'. What was more important was his gleaming red sports car. What would better demonstrate that I was off 'that stuff' than taking this clean-cut young man home to meet my folks in Ballater that summer?

I must be getting sick if I'm having horny dreams! Still, it was only for a few days.

After my trip Down Under, I'd accepted Major Tom wasn't the only junky. Yet despite the label, I still hadn't reached my all-time low … not yet. There was never any question of having to go on the street to turn tricks, shoplift or even beg and borrow from friends for my smack money. I was also still alive, contrary to the BBC documentaries I'd seen, showing working-class mothers crying and weeping over their offspring's heroin-riddled coffins. In fact, after that trip, I had danced on the edge of success.

Terry may have been a fantasy, I'll never know, but *Quadrophenia* was within my grasp. I knew it; they'd even spoken about changing the script for me. Once I sensed they really wanted me, I eagerly leapt in with both boots. I was already in elocution lessons. I'd managed to drop my Doric to a softer, more distinguishable tone; unfortunately, Cockney was just too big a vocal leap. I tried to talk myself up, make myself ready for that third call-back. *They want you; they love you, darling, isn't it obvious? Your accent is fine, no need to worry, the other girls they're auditioning are hideous, fat trolls and trollops, don't let them scare you!* Years ago, Mum on her shoestring budget had taken me to elocution lessons in town so I could fit in at school. It was traumatic: smelly, frizzy hair, wrong address, and now *I can't talk properly!*

There was also something about not wanting to lose the little bit of self I had left.

Back in the early days, I'd taken a trip to Victoria one lunchtime. Hungry, I decided to try the sandwich bar opposite the station. It was a novelty beyond compare, all the boxes filled with every kind of cold meat, fish, pickles, slaws, and cheeses. Even a choice of breads. At that time, the Victoria Tea Rooms in Aberdeen offered a paltry menu: pie, chips and beans or pie, chips and peas, either a ham and mustard or a cheese and tomato sandwich … but let's not forget at least twenty different kinds of disgusting pastel-shaded, cream-filled cakes. Ugh! But what was this here? My imagination roared into overdrive! Senses aroused, I announced to the server:

'A salmon and cucumber sandwich, please.'

'You wot, luv?' he replied, squinting his eyes, not understanding my accent.

'A saaaalmin and kewkumbrrr sandd-wich please.'

'You *wot*, sweetheart?' he repeated, staring me down, daring me.

I was devastated. Several repeats and much pointing later, the embarrassment rising red on my cheeks, and impatience slamming me from behind, his face twisted into a wink and a grin:

'You're alright, Jock, salmon and cucumber on white, coming up!'

I stood there, speechless. I got called Jock a lot, especially by the East End boys at the shop. Always with a brotherly affection and a tinge of bemusement at our national characteristics, including my lilting brogue. If there was an arrogance behind it, I never felt it; for me, any leg-pulling was overshadowed by the warmth. Those differences, well they were the things that made me most proud to be Scottish. I always loved being called Jock; it gave me a sense of belonging. No one would call me Jock now ... but they widna ca' mi 'bleedin' Eliza Doolittle eiva!'

* * *

I'd made a lot of friends in the modelling business: photographers, guys I'd slogged out test shots with back in the early days. One of them asked me to set up a model agency with him. I was starting to get more 'mature work' in advertising, playing a slightly older woman. My agent said to me, 'You'll always get work, Vicki. You've got a good face! You could stay here if you can get clean.'

Get clean? I shuddered with humiliation. *Does everybody know?*

Apparently, they did. I'd been around for a while now as a model and as Marilyn I was well known and well loved. I may have arrived late, spent too long in the bathroom shooting up, sometimes nodded off, but I was a good model, professional and honest and trustworthy. I was getting steady work from all my agencies. Yet it was almost as if, as my career climbed higher, so my junky side sank lower.

It was ironic, paradoxical, crazy! I had friends in the celebrity scene—not that I frequented it often, but I liked to know that I had my place. Society scared me, and I had never been a party girl. The celebrity notches in my bedpost were considerably less than other girls in my position. I had never been attracted by fame, but I loved that it was *there*. And I loved London. I felt I'd earned my residency, made it my home. I loved my flat in Kilburn; Olga and Everett were part of that. The thought of going home to Aberdeen—returning *ever*—felt like a sign of surrender. Defeat. Desperation. An absolute tragedy. Yet the threat of it was never far while my sisters were around.

Then one day I returned from a modelling trip to Hamburg to discover there was a magpie in the nest.

* * *

Born when I was eight, left in nappies far too long, a third baby had sent Mum over the edge. They even referred to her as a 'mistake'—not that it was uncommon for parents to say that back then. It meant *unplanned*, not unwanted, yet still …

As we grew older, Kim and I would speak about her. Trying to figure her out: what we saw as her jealousies, her bitterness, vindictiveness. Even her fake voices— 'Just like Mum. Mum has fake voices, too.' Those behaviours remained unexplained, a mystery. Yet we never questioned why all three of us fought so much. Sisters scrapping over turf seemed normal. How well someone could handle themselves in a scrap was not an unusual conversation. Yet in a family, there were rules.

Happily unpacking in my bedroom after a successful modelling trip to Hamburg doing a massive poster for Kodak, I thought I'd make myself a nice cuppa. As I walked into the lounge, my jaw dropped open and my brain whirred at the weird, incongruent sight—Curly and Lisa close up and cosy on the sofa. Whaaaaaaaaaat!

'What the fuck is this now?'

Looking up with feigned innocence—*laced with spite*, I secretly thought—Lisa replied, 'We've been out to the disco and that. You told him to show me around.'

I suppose I had.

Curly couldn't quite pull that one off though and a 'yes I fucking did' grin broke over his cheeky face.

I stormed out to a backdrop of whining protests: 'You said you were finished with him'.

* * *

'What difference was that supposed to make,' I ruminated. It hurt so deeply, and I wasn't entirely sure why. I mean it wasn't as if Curly and I were exclusive in any way. He took blow jobs as payment in kind from the sex workers all the time. It never bothered me; I'd call him a filthy little bastard and we'd laugh.

Yet now, Curly's betrayal crossed the line. Curly, who'd given me my very first hit and hung around for the next five years, was evicted from my life.

Forever.

Curly and I had never discussed our relationship, nor cared to categorise it. We were simply two junkies from neighbouring estates. Yet this betrayal bothered me so much that even weeks later, I spent hours crying in his bedsit in Paddington, pleading with him to tell me, *Why, why, why?* 'My little sister! How could you? You know how I feel she's weird with me, been a thorn in my side, jealous or whatever, but dammit Curly, she's *my sister!*'

That broke me. He'd never feature on my radar again.

I never asked my sister the same question. It's sad but true how utterly irreparable some rifts are.

Yet for years I tried to overlook it; I loved my sisters. I believed we were part of a whole, a nuclear unit, a family. Flesh and blood and all that. Naturally I thought they must love me, too; the only conclusion I could reach was to ask myself, 'What's wrong with *me*, that a sister would do that?' It seemed to be generally accepted that there *was* something wrong with me. During periods of depression, I'd hunt around inside my head for the elusive answer. I'd replay my life story over … and over … and over again. Rewinding and fast-forwarding desperately to find the truth behind the familial myths.

Mum's story: 'Naebody could pass us by, they a' winted one o' the thick blonde curls fae the little lassie wi' the big brown eyes.'

My grandma's: 'Little limmer clartit ma wa's wi' syrup aff her piece!' 'The bissom locked her granda in the bird hoos!' The time they squatted me at the bus stop for a pee and I went ahead and unleashed a massive poop, just as the congregation filed out of church one Sunday morning.

'Jist full o' devilment,' they said.

Then there was the school myth: clever girl who won't pay attention. The first day I attended, I hated school instantly, so big and so far away from my bedroom. I was dragged away from my mother in tears. And then there was the uniform, three sizes too big because Mum and Dad really couldn't afford to do it any other way. Dear Jesus, the many horrors! The affront of having to wear grey stockings knitted by my grandma, fastened on to my liberty bodice with suspenders and buttons, which always came to bits at some point during the day, and I simply couldn't get back together for myself. Oh, and let's not forget my mother's face when I showed up with them round my ankles, *again*, incredulous that I couldn't get my clumsy fingers to fasten the buttons hand-sewn to within an inch of their life. Then that feeling of pure, unadulterated shame when she'd lift my skirt to fasten them there and then on Albyn Place. It always seemed to happen right at the pedestrian gate, the same place where Kirsty's mother pulled up.

At least Kirsty was worse: big and fat as a cow, with a tangle of black hair. Her mother looked like a witch; as she ushered her charge into the black Morris Minor, sometimes I'd catch a glimpse of their pet raven in the back seat.

We were the weirdos.

The smelly ones.

'Snelling is smelling in the middle of the spelling ...'

In the cloakroom, I knew what that cloakroom meant.

The cloakroom and the rhyme.

Differences flagged up in rhythm.

Memories haunting me through time.

Endless hours under the laburnum tree; why was I so detestable? My hair frizzy from my mother's insistence on brushing my beautiful curls every morning and squishing them under that awful hat. Was I smelly? How would I be able to tell? Maybe that's why nobody liked me. Nobody wanted to play with me.

I hated it.

I hated them.

I hated them for making me go there.

And I hated me.

I was clever though. I could outshine most of them. That felt good. I felt smug and superior in those moments, but it was a small pay-off for hours and days and months of pain and aloneness. I did have my very own hero, though: my dad.

* * *

Dad left school at thirteen, like many in the wartime years. No formal education, he read everything he could lay his hands on, including the classics. In his sixties, he taught himself Spanish. Dad remained sharp as a tack until the day he died. He taught me to read and write with chalk on my blackboard at home and with my finger on the condensation on the Number 22 bus window. I could do it by the time I was three. I can still beat the digital cashier with the mental arithmetic taught to me over endless card games. 'Is she a gifted child?' they all wondered. But Dad knew. He and Mum worked tirelessly and took me on two buses twice a day from Northfield to the West End, so I could acquire the education they so admired and yearned for me to have. And when the complaints started rolling in from school, Dad gave the spinster headmistress—a dragon from another era—several reality checks in my defence.

Sure, they complained about my inattentiveness. I remember it too: lonely days staring at the rain-streaked window pane from the primary classroom, teacher droning on at her desk. My father would ask if I was falling behind.

'No, Vicki's doing well.'

'So, what exactly *is* the problem?'

Shrugs all around. School eventually sent me to a child psychologist, and as Mum reported to all and sundry: 'They couldna figure oot fit wis wrang wi' her, they must've thought there was something wrang at hame, after meeting us they kint fine it wisna 'at, she's jist a problem child!'

Dad's version: 'She's jist being Vicki. You're too smart for them, aren't ye?' he said grinning, his warm brown eyes winking that special wink.

But the boys …

I remember what those bastards did to me! I'd hear them all laughing, calling me a whore to my face, as they tucked in their shirt and zipped up their fly. My body hated that, assaulted in every way, left shrouded in 'the knowing and yet', any positive thoughts drowned out by the negative chatter:

Shame!

Self-hate!

Disgust!

Condemnation!

Lies and half-truths and more lies running like a ticker tape through my mind!

The knowing, and yet …

What was it about me that made everybody think they could hurt me like that?

Why did my own sisters despise me? Why was I rejected in my hour of teenage need by my own mother?

That 'knowing and yet' compelled me to hate myself. Witnessing the self-destruction in disbelief of how I, myself, could know it for what it was—yet still inflict it upon myself.

Unwanted cocks.

Brutalising sweet honey soft flesh and pearly innocence.

Injecting poison into red-blooded veins, as if my body was some dustbin that would magically digest and spew out the putrid waste, like the scarab.

I thought I was a scarab, strong enough to hold the shame of the whole world. It petrified me into two parts: one the charismatic magnet for more, a deeper, more destructive more, and the other shame-filled, shrinking, solidifying, hidden.

And lost.

I pushed it all down and tried to make myself good. I desperately wanted my parents to benefit from my success, to see I had 'made it', that I was worth it. Dad only visited London one time. Mum visited more. We'd go to Trader Vic's, the bistro she loved off Edgware Road after a Saturday morning raking at the outdoor market. I yearned to please her, yet I always wanted to curl up in my junky nest after she'd gone, feeling unseen, unheard, unloved, unworthy. It propelled me back to that day in the clinic, when I swore I'd never forgive her—that day when my secret mind unleashed on her:

I never asked you for any more than the petty things that were easy to give: sweets, pretty clothes, to stay playing a little longer. You even stood up to my father's strict hand on occasion.

But not that day.

That day you refused to give me my dignity. You refused to give me a path back to self-respect and my father's love.

They raped me, they raped me, they raped me, you stupid fucking bitch! Then because of you, they raped me again!

What sodden shame were you sipping in your gin glass that made you turn your back on my soul's begging? I wept inside.

That was how I thought then.

Forgiveness came later.

Forgiveness came with motherhood, and my spiritual quest. Understanding slowly revealed itself, after that. The sodden shame—well, that is *my mother's* hidden story. Maybe her mother's, too. A hurt so deep, a trauma so frozen, the flames of torment so blazing they blind you, rendering you unable to see your own pain—far less another's. Pain that gets passed through generations, misinterpreted as lack of love, twisted into distance and insecurities where there ought to be none, mangled and warped into an unforgivable rift.

A huge part of the age-old struggle of mother and daughter, trauma perpetuates the rift. Here I include everyone yet use the feminine because I believe it is women who will birth this quiet revolution, hold the energy, and allow the alchemy of change.

Much of my own healing came from conversations with other women, most especially my own daughter, Jessica. We committed to bring love and awareness to the most difficult parts of our own process, so that slowly we could let go of the indefinable hurt. Having that experience and sharing this book with her took it further. Thinking of her beloved Granma, Jessica forced me to look at my words again; I am grateful she did. It allowed me to write the whole story, hold the raw anger, move through the blame, and arrive at the love.

And there was plenty of love.

Love for my mother grew with each passing year. I watched her age, so gracefully. Beautiful as ever, a little frail with her small dainty feet, back slightly rounded, and head tilted back as if her neck was tired from holding it up for nine long decades. With fondness I remember the day we leant against the parapet of Dinnet Bridge, looking into her face, highlighted by the warmth of late summer's light. I knew the love between us would never die; that love is always enough. So soft, so strong, so constant. Her love will suckle me long after she is gone; a return never to be repaid. I absorbed every moment of her. Newly diagnosed with Alzheimer's, she spoke of taking power over her own death; she wanted to say her piece when we were quiet and alone.

My mother gave me many gifts. Even in the torture of dementia, she had an intuition that allowed her to see beyond the obvious. The love, advice and support she has given me over all these years—more than sixty-five of them now! Given with grace and love despite what she must have had to put up with—the teenager I was, the half-dead junky I became. All healed through love. Once Mum's filters were gone, the praise started pouring out. How proud she was of my attendance at the High School, my looks, my modelling career, that I'd written a book and told my truth. The fact that I'd hated school would have made no sense to her; that I had hated myself, even less. She loved me unconditionally. That her impulsive, crazy daughter was vulnerable to rape—no, that simply would not have crossed her mind. No one could touch me; I was the golden child.

But that day when she showed up on West End Lane with Lisa and her look, all I remember thinking was here she is with another she.

CHAPTER TWELVE

Revelations

J ust when it seemed things couldn't get worse …
Just when it seemed my life couldn't become more
twisted and tangled with shame and misery …

Just when it seemed my heart couldn't bear another
hardship or humiliation …

Just when it seemed that something had to give …

It did.

* * *

I couldn't remember the last time I had a period; being a
heavy user, I hadn't even considered that I might be
pregnant. There were no obvious signs: no morning
sickness, no swollen breasts, no bizarre food cravings. I'd
gone to the doctor for something else entirely and suddenly
there it was: 'Around twenty weeks,' he announced,
pointing to my belly. 'Do you have a plan?'

A plan? For what? I suddenly felt light-headed. There
was no plan for anything in my life beyond the next fix.

Unplanned doesn't even begin to describe the tiny
helpless being now growing in my belly. And yet, I

wanted this baby, an unexpected, unasked-for, precious gift suddenly living inside of me. I thought it through: I was financially sound, physically fit, a responsible adult ... *You can do this, Vicki!* I'd be Ms. Scott, like one of those trendy New York businesswomen. There was room enough in my garden flat in Kilburn for an au pair to move in. It was the first time I had dreamt of a different future; I loved it, my heart knew I needed it, and I went straight on to methadone without a second thought.

I recall those glorious weeks with such clarity! Buying maternity clothes, going from not having a clue I was pregnant to proudly showing off my baby bump, making plans for my flat and garden. My sister Kim came to the antenatal appointment with me. Driving there in my little blue Mini we giddily conversed. Kim pleaded to know who the father was: 'What is it to you? You're a nosy one for the world's worst dark horse!' Kim laughed, but in my head I was dodging the same question. 'What difference does it make anyway? It's *my* baby, end of!'

I can see the room at the clinic, the different waiting rooms, the blue and white flowery maternity blouse I wore, complete with Peter Pan collar. I felt so fresh! My hair was bouncy and full of life, my face glowing. I was present, awake, happy and alive in an altered universe.

Meanwhile, the flat got gutted; even Mr E tidied himself up, positively glowing at the prospect of a baby coming into the house. Olga too—we were all full of the joys. It was springtime, the sun beamed through the blinds, birds sang in the garden. I was kneeling by the coffee table, tidying out the secret drawer while mentally going through all the changes I'd have to make, and how I could manage until I went back to work.

The couple upstairs had given me the number for a nanny agency. I could get a French au pair so my baby would be bilingual, or a proper British one with a uniform. *Maybe I'd start a model agency,* I told myself. *I could do that from home, probably get some mother and baby work, too.*

The ringing of the phone startled me from my reverie. I sat back on the hearth to gaze out the window as I picked up. 'Hello? Who's this?' I thought it was a heavy breather at first—but no, the unfamiliar voice was menacing. And it was threatening me. I caught my breath and held it long enough to feel the shot of adrenaline straight to the heart. *Terry. Terry had put a contract on me. The bastard!*

Shocked and angry, I banged the phone down and whirled to face Kim. There had only been one conversation with Terry since Dubai. 'No, I'm *not* giving the money back! I bought the tickets, went to all that trouble …' and then *click!* he hung up … Kim looked at me, I looked back at her, the colour draining from my face as I blurted out the caller's warning.

'That was Terry's hitman!'

'*Whaaat?*'

'Terry's fucking hitman!'

'You better pay him back, Vicki!'

Fuck me, I knew she was right. But how? Terry had been very much on my mind for the past three weeks … *constantly* on my mind, as he had to be my baby's dad.

'*Vickiii!*' Kim's voice brought me back to reality again. 'Pay the man!'

'No way, that's maintenance money!'

She scowled. 'Fuck's sake, girl, wise up!'

I scowled too. *Humph, so he wanted to play dirty, did he?*

'Right'—Kim sighed, seeing my indecision, snatching the phone—'if you won't do something, I'll tell the cops …'

'You can't do that!'

A siren voice blared in my head: *FUCK TERRY!*

'But I fucking will!'

I did. The very next day I marched straight into Edgware Road police station and asked for Special Branch.

'Why do you want Special Branch, madam?'

'An arms dealer has put a contract on me, and I'm pregnant!'

That was how I met Nick.

* * *

A few mornings later I awoke, and as I had done every day for weeks, I put my hands on my belly. Expecting to feel the squishy warmth of my watery gut, I reeled. It was brick hard—something was seriously wrong.

In a panic I called the doctor, then drove myself to the hospital on Marylebone Road. Fearing the worst, I had tests done, and waited. They told me my baby had died. 'You'll still have to give birth,' the doctor explained, 'and I'm afraid for now you won't be getting any methadone.'

Hearing his words, a dark cloud of shame encircled me. My mind shut down, went on autopilot. I guess they induced labour. I'll never know why I didn't look at my baby. I am so ashamed to say that I lied to everyone about it, pretended I did. The doctor told me the cord was wrapped around its neck. I didn't believe him, of course it was my fault.

The despair was deep. The dream was over. My spiral into drugs had stolen the life of something sacred. In emotional pain, I took the kitchen scissors and chopped off my hair. No longer could I pretend I was a responsible adult; I was a limp and slimy addict. Craving more punishment, I only went out for the big-paying Marilyn jobs. That trip to Scotland was an epi crisis, a fake healing, no more. A play act for Mum and Dad that I returned from without hope. My own child had vacated my body. I was putrid and beyond redemption. I rolled around in self-remorse. Took myself to the edge with constant fixing, often waking up, mortuary cold on the bathroom floor, body icy as marble. I had no recollection of the drifting: nothing, a blank, after just wondering where I'd been that I could be so freezing, so chilled to the bone … Was I dead? Was that it, the silence of death, unknown and unknowable? Deep silence, not even a memory. Just cold unconsciousness. A numbness that was becoming all too familiar.

I needed the sun. I needed to get away. I needed warmth.

I flew to Tenerife.

A Dutch property developer I'd been seeing since he jumped off his yacht replete in white slacks (penis profile on display) and Gucci loafers was my first toxic rescuer. Cheeky bastard that he was, he invited himself to join me for coffee. I'd been sitting alone at a harbour-front cafe reading my book. I always enjoyed time on my own, a good novel as the perfect companion. Full of the entitlement of being stinking rich, he came and nosed his way in. He was an interesting character though; I'd enjoyed our chat until he started melting my brain with business talk. We had a fling, and he came in handy in a holiday home kind of way, always having a car and a plush apartment waiting for me when I fancied some sun.

Kim was with me that first trip; we nicknamed the Dutchman 'Whistler'. I'll never forget how Kim nearly wet herself when we shared 'first time' gossip the morning after. We had a ritual for it:

'Well?'

'Nothing.'

'*Come* on!'—*giggles*—'tell me what happened!'

'No, I canna, I canna …' *Hysterics.*

By the time the teasing got to the nips, pokes, and nudges stage we were both hysterical.

'He was whistling at ma fanny!' I struggled to get the words out past the laughter.

'Fit—fuck right off!' Yup, Whistler would pause mid-fuck to whisk his specs on so that he could see my pussy better. Then he'd wolf whistle at it, whip his specs back off again, and get back on the job!

This trip had no humour though. I was burnt out, and Whistler left me to it.

The second night in, I started to lose it. Coated in sweat, I'd managed to squeeze myself between the back of the sofa and the wall. It was where I'd chosen to lay trembling that put me over the edge. Not my shit-streaked, sweaty joggers. Not the baby whose soul had touched mine then moved on to a better place. Not the sister who had betrayed me, nor the best friend who abandoned me. Not the fact that I knew I was squeezing the last out of Abdul and he would soon leave me too. None of that. But how could I lie there behind that settee, hugging the wall like that, sweat gushing from my every pore, my brain thrashing in its lunatic single-mindedness? *I want heroin. I want a fix. Now!*

I zoned out for a while. A blissful reprieve: maybe I had slept. I'd slept the night before. Yet I knew I wouldn't sleep tonight. I pulled my knees to my chest against the pulsating throbbing cramps in my stomach. Fuck, they hurt! There were moments of time passing; then the retching started. More cramps, deeper shivering, a colder sweat. I was scared; I'd never gone this far. What was I thinking? I had nothing, not even a sleeper. How bad was it going to get? In another moment's quiet I marvelled at the goosebumps; they were an actual thing: 'Cold turkey has got you ... on the run.' It's real, there they were on my arm, rising as I gazed in disbelief. It's happening! Sweating! Painful shivering! Too cold to ever heat up! *I'll never make it. My habit's too huge. My time is up.*

I had a lot of pain to push down.

The maze of mental anguish was the worst of it. I could go out to find a score, but I was weak—and what would there be to score in Tenerife anyway? If I went to the local hospital, they'd lock me up. My mind screamed and my legs kicked. There was no rest from it. I wanted to crawl out of my own skin. All that focused desire to get clean was a lie, pitched in a losing battle against my weak self-control. *Why are you bothering? You weren't ever going to get clean anyway! You're finished as a model; everyone is sick of you.*

Gathering my Moschino belt to place around my neck and my vanity case to stand on, I wandered dizzily into the bathroom.

The picture my brain had shown me of my body dangling over the bath was more appealing than the shivering, sweating, incontinent woman curled on the floor. She was lying there miserable, full of shame, wanting to die.

I'd attempted coming off before; this was the first and last time I tried to take my life. Luckily it was the shower fitting that snapped and not my neck. *Pathetic. Stupid cunt. Can't even off yourself properly.* Somehow, I staggered out the door. Not knowing where to put myself I left that apartment and walked and walked and walked.

I walked past the horny skulking youths waiting outside the nightclubs. Past the empty suburban streets with couples and children sleeping on their carved mahogany beds. I walked through the night and into the dawn, barely conscious of where I was going. At last, I stumbled into some open space. A wasteland soon to be more apartment blocks. In a stupor, the bitter sting of my own self-contempt came flooding back: my entire life was a wasteland!

The realisation, the unbearable weight of it all bore down on my drug-weakened mind. I stumbled through the enormous vacant urban space, reeling with images of my disgrace. As the sun appeared over the hills ahead of me, I choked back a wave of unexpected remorse.

Suddenly, out of nowhere, a voice jarred me, startled me, thundering in my ears:

'You can be reborn,' it said.

The words slammed into me like a hurricane. *Reborn?* Tears flowed from my eyes. I felt my heart pounding—pounding so loud, so hard that my neck throbbed. For a moment I couldn't breathe in or out. As my brain took in the message, I experienced a feeling of joy so profound, so stirring, so filled with love and hope and promise that my life pivoted on its heel at that exact moment.

What if? I asked myself. *What if it was true? What if all I believed about myself was a lie? What if I could be reborn? What if I could embrace the freeing affirmation of a new start, a new life?*

What if?

Stunned and staring into the sun now I stood frozen, unable to hear anything but the pounding of my own blood in my ears. All my life I'd felt like a misfit, left out in the cold. My depression was suddenly transformed into a new sense of power. My attempt at cold turkey and suicide had ended in the first of many spiritual experiences that altered the course of my life. It didn't happen overnight. I still hadn't found what I was looking for. That would take time, many years. But that was the beginning.

* * *

With Whistler's help, I left Tenerife the next day and flew straight to my dealers. *Just one more score until I got my head together,* I promised myself. I didn't have what it took for cold turkey; I might as well be honest with myself. I'd need to find another way.

I tried rehab next.

Somewhere south of London, I found a small clinic with a pool table, a dispensing centre, canteen, craft rooms and lots and lots of time. I made friends on the first night with another inmate, an ex-bum boy; he was so pretty, in a male model kind of way, with his blonde waves and baby blues. I could see why all the men drooled after him. I assumed he was gay and was surprised when our friendship got steamy. Pretty hilarious, when I look back on it: the rule was that you could sit on each other's beds so long as one foot was on the floor. Are you *mad?!* Bizarre. Rehab wasn't all bad. I shagged my way through it, made a few other friends, and finally had the time to learn how to play pool.

I'd even got past that place where methadone was just not hitting the spot. Of course, as every addict knows, that is the point you get offered a score. There's no turning back an addicted mind from that offer, even when you don't really want the crap gear you know you're going to end up with, nor the disappointment and regret you know is going to come with it. The mind's already there, begging you to inject the poison into your bloodstream, tugging at your sleeve. The rendezvous was the back window; most of us had some.

That killed rehab for me.

Pretty boy and I took to the road, kidding ourselves that we were going to go travelling to get clean. It wasn't the first time I'd told myself that one. The alternative was going back to London and the life we both wanted to escape and steer clear of.

We tried.

Hitching south to the ferry, we popped the pocketful of pills Pretty had taken along. I was stuck-up about my gear, and pills were not my thing, but on this occasion, something was better than nothing. I have no recollections whatsoever of that journey. The next thing I remember was walking up a hill in Barcelona, seemingly in the opposite direction of the tourists headed out for a night on the razz. That's how we met Lyall and his mates. At first glance I thought of Lyall as a lager lout; that was his general appearance, but he soon broke away from his mates and tagged along with us.

Barcelona was filled with wild, drunken highs. A good-looking pair, Pretty and I got free entry and were bought drinks wherever we went—and if not, Lyall was there to pick up the tab. My memories are mere glimpses of outrageous behaviour, skanking whatever was needed or simply because we could. It was fun having a male counterpart.

Lyall stayed on when his mates left and took a room at our pensione with us. One day as I lay stretched out on our bed, Lyall came through and asked to borrow the off-the-shoulder, cave girl leopard-skin dress I'd worn the night before. *Yikes!* Mind you, Lyall was a huge guy. I had heaps of tranny mates in London, but I hadn't twigged Lyall's deal, nor, it seemed, did he realise it's a girl rule that you just don't ask to borrow THE best dress. The dress was hot, one of my favourites ever. I liked Lyall and didn't want him to feel bad, but it was hard work feigning pleasure watching him get off on his personal floor show later that evening. I'm not sure if he was hoping Pretty would give him one; that didn't happen anyway, but we did let him stay and watch us fuck while he had a wank.

As colourful a threesome as we were, it jaded quickly for me. I can't remember if Pretty was epileptic and had run out of meds, or if perhaps it was the cocktail he'd been given at rehab. I do remember the Spanish accident and emergency giving him Largactil. Anyway, he was fitting all over the place and the dramas were coming thick and fast now. I'd had enough and called someone to credit card me out of there. The mixture of drugs, anxiety and uncertainty was too much, I needed a break. I needed to get drunk to sleep, yet remain aware enough to look out for the two crazies with me, neither of whom seemed to have much thought beyond the next high.

I was on the edge of a breakdown. I desperately wanted home to my lovely dealer and some Persian brown.

Sadly, even Toni was not the same. My long-time Persian friend was living with Shirley. I'd introduced them; I thought they might boost each other up, but it hadn't worked. Shirley was doing second-rate escort work, and Toni seemed to have gotten lazy. Whatever the cause he was losing his touch—he looked ill, drawn, tired. His smack was not so great. 'Can't seem to find the good stuff anymore,' he yawned through dirty teeth. Toni and I had shared some good gear and some good chat, including his memories from the old Persia.

Looking back at my life then, I saw only a few bright hours between seasons of darkness. And now another part of my story was coming to an end.

* * *

When I wasn't forced to work, I was just passing time. If I wasn't sitting talking rubbish with the junkies next door, chasing the dragon because we were all running out of veins, I'd be compulsively tidying my portfolios in the office or maybe cleaning out my make-up box. I'd also developed this habit of counting—'One two three four five six seven, all good child-ren go to heaven'—as I washed out my works in the white sink in the brown bathroom while watching the blood diluting then running down the plug hole. It had to be at least seven times. On the days I shoved my ten grand fox fur over the top of my joggers, grabbed the supermarket trolley that had permanent residence in my back garden, and pushed it down the high street gathering chocolate biscuits and other junk food, I always avoided the cracks in the pavement. Sometimes I'd stop at the penny arcade. If I went in there, hours would pass; I might still be there when either cold, hunger or the need for another fix would force me home again. Sometimes I would find out if Olga was free, and we'd spend all afternoon in the bingo.

Then Eddie moved in for a while.

I liked staying home with Eddie. Eddie had been Curly's friend, we'd often been a foursome, so when he split up with his long-term girlfriend, it seemed natural that we'd get together. Half Greek, brown eyes, fine nose, tall and handsome, Eddie had a placid nature and we got on well, so our life together held no major challenges. He'd go out for gear when we needed it, someone else would pick up the

Big Macs, and we'd huddle around in joggers shooting up and watching movies. No pretending anymore.

The options I saw laid before me were not enticing; in fact, they looked like a menu from hell.

Much as I would have liked to stay in my home near my friends, my career, and the life I'd carved out of nothing, deep in my heart I knew that time was running out. I'd have to give up the London I'd grown up in and loved deeply. I needed to let go of my ambition of maturing into an actress and businesswoman, the one that was healthy and looked a little like that pregnant me. I didn't have what it took to cross the bridge into that future.

I was thirty now, and I had always said I'd give it a number. That was wise. I wouldn't want to be reminded daily of the ravages of time and how that somehow made you 'less'. I'd noticed a colleague, a few years my senior, with her little sticky pads of a facelift. There were other types of ageing that cameras couldn't see. Not for me, sister! But even that was a lie, because deep inside I prayed that the day would come when I'd be good enough, that the actress I felt inside would come bursting out, that the accent I asked for would wiggle its way from my brain, through my throat and into a voice that portrayed the feelings inside of me.

Someone would notice. And they did. And they had.

But me—never trusting, always scared, never willing to give myself in that way, terrified to go to the core, to reach deep enough—never, ever me.

Those early years on my £25 pushbike with my portfolio strapped to the side, pedalling Chelsea, Putney, Fulham, Soho and North-West One, now came roaring back at me. Beautiful pictures were created: I saw my beauty reflected in their eyes, in what I could stir up inside them, but it was never quite right for where I wanted to go. Good for the glamour shots, maybe, which the negative chatter in my head translated into '*Not good enough for anything else.*' I kept trying; there was a quiet voice inside that pushed me on, and anyway I was young, and life was fun. I made Page 3 of *The Sun*, the *Daily Mirror*, the motor show. Recognition! Renown! Prestige! Popularity! But then I went and got myself in a mess: a love that was bound for rejection and a retreat that led me into the arms of a homeboy and his heroin habit.

Even after that I still had hope. The way they really tried to mould me for the leading role in *Quadrophenia*, how Ronnie Barker drew the comedienne out of me, and what was becoming slow but steady work for the Beeb. At last, I was part of it! There were times it didn't pay the way, but something always came round the corner. There were offers of running model agencies, encouragement that my face was good enough to still be getting ad work in my forties. But the heroin had injected itself deep into my soul; it had become part of who I was, or so I thought:

'And then one day you'll find ten years have gone behind ...'

I woke up after my second child was lost, and part of me died too. I was a shell, just working for my habit, papering over the cracks.

And there were many cracks. Too many to fill.

The final push came from Kim. She spilled to Mum and Dad that I wasn't clean at all. I couldn't bear their fear and hurt. I sold my flat, and at the age of thirty, I was now a retired model, not rich, but with enough not to need to worry. It was painful. I'd strived for my London home, decorated each corner with love, filled it with mementos from my journeys around the world. All given away in an opiate stupor; gas fires to keep the junky next door's kids cosy, a fur coat to keep a home girl warm on the streets, leopard skin rugs, jewellery, clothes and furniture. Even the crockery, all given away.

There was one way out of this. Kim wove me a fantasy: my next incarnation was to be Zoe Zonnar, hotshot lawyer! I took it, signed up for college and loaded with Harley Street methadone, returned to Aberdeen in August 1987.

Kim's alternative reality got me out of London and through a law degree. The law degree distracted me enough to wean myself off methadone. But this wasn't my dream—it was a nightmare that I didn't have the backbone to end. I was back where I started, the place I'd done everything to run away from. What happened to my hutzpah, my brass neck? I didn't have any backbone at all! And the single most recurring image I had of myself during withdrawing from opiates was that of a jellyfish.

Spineless! Fragile! Drifting through life! The bastards had destroyed my shell. Burying my pain, I steeled myself to walk the fifty yards to the paper shop. I counted the sapling larch wondering at the ugliness of their grey supports with dull metal straps. I needed something like that. It was terrifying just walking down the street. I was carrying my pain on a display board in front of me. Anyone could walk up to me and kick it hard.

I had become numb to life, without any clue what to do about it. That was the first stage. As the numbness melted, the terror crept in—but that was nothing compared to what happened when my emotions finally broke free of their chains and escaped from jail.

* * *

I continued with my pitiful reductions for three years of two steps forward and one step back. My self-imposed sentence was interspersed with trips to my Harley Street quack and the odd modelling job. Obviously, that also meant a trip to Edgeware Road for a score. Eventually I got there though. I managed to occupy the galloping rant in my brain with studying. I pacified the cravings with the fat and sugar in the 'Aberdeen roll' I set out to buy each day. *If I limit my other doses,* I promised myself, *I can get a large scoof of methadone later and enjoy a good gouch in the afternoon.*

Yes, I know lots about self-abuse, but being a junky also gave me relentless single-mindedness. A friend I met at university, Gail, helped me develop a new addiction: fitness. That, and an awareness of nutrition, slowly sorted out the physical damage from sugar and smack. My mum told me about an acupuncturist and dragged me along to Transcendental Meditation. I'm not even certain I can remember doing it those first three years, but I did, and once my body found its fitness again and the chemical rampage began to settle down, I noticed a growing peace, a calm. Then one day, I spied the buds on one of those larch, and realised life could renew itself.

And if it could, so could I.

Awareness kind of crept up on me after that, although there have been many times when I wished I could put it back!

Law, now mastered, was a bit of a bore, but the challenge of getting high enough marks to get to Palermo University for the spring term spurred me on.

Then came Sicily … amazing! Sicily's contradictions fascinated me: monasteries and convents with electronic gates paid for with Mafia money, phallic graffiti on the road to holy monuments. The images in my mind of blood-stained virgin sheets just a blink of an eye away; raw sexuality, fear, corruption, all watched over by the Blessed Virgin.

And there I was, the oddball amongst thirty snogging university kids. Many of them were sixteen going on forty, privately educated and weighed down by expectation before they'd even experimented with life. Poor brainwashed babies! Yet I felt so vulnerable beside them. At least they were certain. I was becoming aware of how different I appeared on the outside compared to how I was on the inside. They knew I was an ex-model, a good-looking woman with a certain amount of celebrity. I'd found my own apartment in a Mondello backstreet, driven my little Renault 5 over from Scotland, had guys taking me out on their speed boats for delicious Italian dinners. Little did they know that long after they collapsed into bed I sat alone in the all-night cafe, munching Valium, sleepers, and painkillers chased by brandy-laced coffee and fags to dull the noise of teeth rotting under expensive crowns, bones screaming for mercy and a voice crying that I'd never make it anyway. Yes, methadone got deeper into my bones than the smack itself. It was a horrible, slow, insidious withdrawal. *When would I ever be able to completely let it go?*

It happened close to the day that Italy beat Argentina during the 1990 World Cup—what a day that was in Mondello Square, with the cars all honking and hooting, such a wonderful atmosphere! That day, I swallowed the very last drop.

CHAPTER THIRTEEN

Sicilian Paradise

L ago di Garda … my heart bursts into giddy excitement just at the sound of it!

Mum had been over holidaying: sunbathing, eating prawns and shopping. My landlord—Santino, a sometimes charming, sometimes grumpy old fisherman—like everyone else in the village, had half a dozen seasonal jobs. Because Mum loved nothing more than a good dish of grilled garlic prawns and a glass of wine, on her first night out we sauntered by the restaurant where Santi shucked oysters: '*Ciao, bella, questa deve essere tua sorella?*'

'*Si, Stronzo!*' The three of us laughed, Mum had no clue what at, but understood that the rugged old Sicilian was flirting with her, flashing his dark eyes admiringly in her direction.

'*Mangia, mangia?*' He glanced back at me.

'*Non ancora, Santi.*'

'*Dai, apri e mangia.*' We did, our taste buds eagerly awaiting what was guaranteed to be the most delicious of fresh oysters.

'*Grazie mille.*'

Mum and I were having a great time: sweet pastries with cappuccino for breakfast, walking along the beautiful seafront and lazing in the sun. Those fishermen in good enough shape were doing their summer stint as bodyguards, and we enjoyed their company: charming, hunky, attentive, giving us the VIP treatment—free sunbeds, changing huts, service with a smile. There was only one thing I loved more than the beach burger van's vege alternative—melanzane alla parmigiana in a bun, *yum!*—and that was watching Fede, the gorgeous lifeguard, run up to the kiosk *Baywatch*-style to put in our order …

That was until the day Santi came running to get me—my sisters had called the restaurant in a panic. Dad had suffered a heart attack. It was all I could do to get Mum on a flight, heart in my mouth and hands shaking while pretending it wasn't that serious.

Luckily it wasn't. Dad was going to survive and did for twenty-nine more happy years.

Never one to look a gift horse in the mouth, I snatched the opportunity to drive my car back from Scotland so I could do a little exploring. Picking up hitchhikers for company and to get a break from driving was how I met Franco. Chivalrous, while filling up with petrol and cappuccino, Franco suggested his friend could drive his car and he mine so I could have a rest. I wasn't surprised. Franco's family owned a hotel on a lake not far from where I'd crossed the Swiss border, so I took a little detour to stay a few days relaxing, eating good food and cruising on his motorboat. That was when the chat got around to water-skiing.

One of the guys I'd been dating in Sicily owned a superfast speedboat; another friend—Orazio, one of the fishermen—knew someone in his bay who possessed a pair of water-skis and a rope. That was good enough. I was there at every opportunity.

One day while out on the bay I noticed Ori waving his arms manically in the air. I looked down to see an entourage of dolphins playing just next to my skis. It was incredible, one of the most amazing encounters of nature I have ever experienced.

Alas, soon it was time to leave my Sicilian paradise: Mondello with its beach, its hot and cold rock pools hidden in nature, the sweetest baby fruits ever, hand fed to me during a romantic date with a gorgeous dentist. Stromboli, for me the Garden of Eden if there ever was one, where I slept two nights in a cave with an Italian/German couple and learnt how to cook my now world-famous Stromboli pasta on a camping stove. The restaurant at the foot of Mount Etna where I ate crab pasta for the first time ever. Even my final farewell to Santi had its poignant moment. Santi had sworn at me in Sicilian for the whole four months I stayed in his upstairs apartment. I was only grappling with get-by Italian, Sicilian, no chance. Knowing I was frustrated at never having a comeback, Santi wound me up every time he saw me. Sometimes I'd swear at him in Italian, but no, that wasn't cutting it. He'd put on his grumpy face, shrug his shoulders, say '*Non capisce,*' and walk away muttering something about foreigners. I practised for hours to get my parting shot perfect; after the initial shock he was so proud of my delivery, we laughed and hugged, our paths never likely to cross again, just memories of time well spent: *la dolce far niente!*

At Franco's suggestion I headed to Lago di Garda, Tracy Chapman blaring out of my open windows:

You got a fast car
I want a ticket to anywhere
Maybe we make a deal
Maybe together, we can get somewhere
Any place is better
Starting from zero, got nothing to lose
Maybe we'll make something
Me, myself, I got nothing to prove ...

And I didn't. I was alive—no, for the first time I was *living!* Marvelling at the sights, stopping to explore vineyards, happening upon a restaurant straight out of *The Godfather* where—having no idea what I was eating—I had my first taste of truffles. Finally reaching my destination, I pitched my tent next to the water-ski school, determined to stay put until I managed to get out of the water on one ski—a skill that had proven impossible with the makeshift rig up in Sicily. The effort had toned my already fit body, and the sport became my passion for the next twenty years. That night I lay in my sleeping bag, in awe of Mother Nature as I watched the most magnificent storm crossing the lake, and wondered what life had in store for me next.

Suntanned, rested and with a little Italian chic I returned to Aberdeen and settled into university life. Dismissing any thoughts of becoming a solicitor, I took the honours degree, thus opening the door to more interesting subjects. I began to love academic life. My hours were my own. Mornings I'd go to the gym, the exhibitionist in me loving to strut into the weights room, doing twelve chin-ups cold, knowing every single male in the place was gawping at me. I imagined their lusty whispers: 'Ooh, I like her tits in that top!' 'Lovely tits they are, all sweaty …' 'And look at that arse! What I'd give to get my nose in them knickers!'

'You're a sick prick, you are!' Impressed or terrified, it didn't matter; I revelled in it. Iron duly pumped, I'd sip an espresso, drag on two or three successive Marlboros, grab brunch, then head for home via the law library to study for the rest of the day.

Home—the first I could call my own since leaving London—was a top-floor one-bed flat at the edge of the city. From the window I could glimpse the countryside.

Quiet and clean, it served my return to the ordinary world well.

When a would-be suitor (and there were quite a few hopefuls on the list) showed up on Valentine's Day, flaunting a pair of chipmunks imprisoned in a fish tank, I was aghast! They were beautiful little animals; what heartless soul would ever lock up innocent creatures of the wild like that? Naturally, my cruel Romeo got the boot, and my furry new companions Mork and Mindy moved in. They shared the lounge with its antique desk in the corner, massive sofa and coffee table, and I made them a climbing frame throughout the area with small hazel trees I'd cut down in the woods. The chipmunks scurried around as they pleased, seeking out the little pine kernels I'd concealed here and there for them. Mork—displaying battle scars from fighting off other males—sat on my head as I studied. This meant I was either plonking away on the Amstrad I'd bought for a few pounds or sitting on the floor stretching while reading through the research. Supposedly untameable, the chipmunks became quite domesticated; Mork even got into the habit of scampering through to the bedroom to wake me in the morning. 'Thank you, Mork, my darling! Now bugger off and let me sleep!' I was so proud of my new playmates, and not just about that: at the age of thirty-five, I could do the splits for the first time in my life! I also managed to keep house without a cleaner—who knew! I was even starting to have days where I felt happy and free.

Having disconnected from all old friends—a sad but essential move—I now had a new gang. Friday nights were for clubbing. Saturday was date night, and Sundays we'd drive thirty miles from Aberdeen to the water-ski club in Aboyne where we'd ski at least three times without fail, so that our butts were pert and toned for the skin-tight bootleg jeans we squeezed into for the weekend's essential moment: Sunday at Mr G's!

By the time I graduated in 1992, between the focus gained from meditation, a body that adored fitness and a vegetarian diet, I looked more like a gladiator than a Page 3 girl. I was ten stones of solid muscle and wore size 8 jeans. My aura as bent, twisted, and shadowed from years of abuse was now beginning to glow. The process of awakening had begun.

So had dating. I had a little black book many women would have given their eye teeth for, and a degree in law. Fitness brought me a physical strength I'd never known before, and from that and my journey to inner strength through spiritual development came two longings: for love, and for a child to be born of that love.

Enter Bill.

* * *

Having opened the door, and put out the invitation to the universe, this is what happened.

While I was enjoying my single status, along with the liberation of being drug-free, I had been thinking about it—my soulmate. I remember saying to Fifi as we drove to Aboyne one weekend:

'I've written my list for my perfect man.'

'What, something more than a big cock?'

'Shut up! I'm being serious. If I meet a guy who's good-enough-looking, a good enough earner without being all up himself and expecting me to be all over him, shares the chores, respects my beliefs, and is decent enough in the sack, I'd like to have a baby with him.'

'Straight up? So, what if you don't meet Mr Right? What then?'

'Well, then I'm going to be an academic lawyer in a top university and be assured of a bevy of young toy boys just for fun!'

We giggled the rest of the road to Aboyne putting arms, legs and other appendages on that one. Nevertheless, *that* was the plan.

I'd been writing wish lists long before I'd read Louise Hay or heard of Tony Robbins. I guess you could say I was always a natural when it came to magic and witchcraft. Even in childhood, my sisters and I made up spells, so it didn't take long before someone came along to fit the 'bill'.

I met him two days after graduation. I still have the photograph. I'd grown my hair, something I wanted to do for such a long time but couldn't because of modelling and wigs. After five years in Aberdeen, it was almost to my waist and left to its own wild natural curls. Standing in that graduation photograph with my mum and dad, knowing how proud they were, I could have burst with happiness. I had been fully clean for more than two years. My body was strong, my mind beginning to calm; I felt spiritually connected. My past gave me a boldness and confidence I didn't see in others. Life was fun again. I felt alive; I could conquer anything! I was even starting to like myself.

Then Bill came into the picture.

Donald, a friend who'd kept in touch throughout the London years, was a DJ at Mr G's. Fifi and I were there with him celebrating my graduation when I spotted the boy with the intense stare. It didn't matter that his boyish prettiness was fading, brushed over by the thinning hair on his soon-to-be-bald head; that's not what I saw in him. There was something in his longing that matched mine. I stood up in the DJ box, showed him my boobs and we ended up in Donald's spare bed. I remember thinking, *He'll do for the winter ... if I come home.* In the morning, as the taxi dropped me off at my little soft-top Suzuki Jeep, he asked me for my number. As I wrote it out, quite oblivious as to how smitten he was, I said nonchalantly: 'I'm going to Greece tomorrow, I'll be back in October.'

Fifi, who looked after the flat and nannied for Mork and Mindy while I was gone, said on one of our weekly phone calls: 'That wanker phoned again at three in the morning when he was drunk!' She was talking about Bill.

Much to her annoyance, I replied: 'Just give him the ski club number, that should get him off your case.'

It didn't.

After several more late-night calls, Bill plucked up the courage and called me in Greece, struggling his way through small talk. Finally, he asked, 'What're you doing this winter?'

'Plan is to go to Canada in 1993 to do a research master's: my dissertation has been published and I've been offered a $20,000 scholarship on the back of it, so I think I'll look for work in Aberdeen this winter to top up those funds.'

Bill's instant reply was: 'Oh, I'm going to South America,' and just like that, the one-upmanship that persisted our whole relationship began.

I had no cynical voice within saying, *This guy's just trying to impress.* If I had, it might have given me a giggle, but I was too literal for that. Nor was there a feminist voice warning, *Beware, he's not acknowledging your achievement!* I had absolutely zilch understanding of the complicated issues that led me to this place and how easily I could be triggered by any hint of rejection. I knew Bill was showing off, yet my strongest feeling was, *He doesn't sound that interested.* That's how I felt despite the drunken calls and desperado landline shouts to the Greek Islands …

Even if the goddess herself had screamed from the hilltops: '*Codependency alert!*' I would have thought she was talking about two junkies jacking up together; nothing to do with the new healthy me and the superficially straight-laced country boy I was about to hitch my wagon to.

It was that split within me, always believing myself to be the baddie, the shrewd one. If that was the case, then it followed that everyone else from the Scotland I'd left behind must be on the good guy team. Yet I must admit I did feel the sting of his retort. I felt it in my gut, but had no clue what it was, only a general feeling of being overlooked, perhaps a slithering suspicion of a lie. I decided to ignore it.

The knowing, and yet …

I suppose it was feasible that Bill's job could take him to South America; however, the energy of the statement just wasn't right. I didn't spend too much time thinking about it; why would I when I was living one of the hedonistic high spots of my life?

Fifi, Donald and I had discovered the Greek Island of Poros during a quick pre-graduation holiday. An hour's ride on the Delfini from Athens, it housed a water-ski school favoured by millionaires from Athens and was staffed by hunky international champions. On the weekends the jet set would arrive on their yachts, and all the beautiful people from the ski club would climb aboard and visit a new port or island for dinner. Someone would foot the bill for all twenty or thirty of us without any expectation for afters or even worries of them. There were plenty of willing and nubile young lovelies more than happy to oblige.

Accommodation: a show apartment rent-free courtesy of a friend's brother who owned the building site. Transport: long-term hire of a moped. Dress code: teeny-tiny bikinis, cut-offs and bare feet.

I was living the dream!

I'd help at the club for free skis, sell pendants on the beach in the afternoons, and work at the bar downtown on the weekends. My workmate—the gorgeous half-Greek, half-Swiss wife of one of the skiers—and I would boogie on the bar, get our boobs out and pour shots. It was THE place to be. After our shift, the crowd would grab a hold wherever they could on her Alfa Romeo Spider as we zoomed to the clifftop nightclub to dance the rest of the night away. The after-party? A secluded beach not far from the ski club where bodies mingled and made love under the Greek stars. What else?

The weeks of sun, fun, fitness and bonhomie passed easily.

I did have a little soft spot for one of the Sun Sail crew. At the end of the season, along with his boss's son—a beautiful blue-eyed Greek—we returned one of the yachts to Thessalonica. That was a beautiful voyage. Life was good and full of fun so why would I suspect that the boy waiting back home was about to become my nemesis? No, I was too wrapped up in bliss playing in the Greek sun that whole wonderful summer, and Bill's psyche was not on my list of things to think about.

That all came much later.

I would have been equally happy to ignore my own darkness, but as you know it doesn't work that way, and beneath the pleasure, the anger and frustration that covers up deep pain had started to come out to play, too. Most of it was channelled grappling with the slalom course; I even barefooted around the bay, but there were also barroom fights. I ended up outside in the alley next to our bar with the girl who not only dared to check out my toy boy but flashed her French daggers at me when I took up a proprietorial stance. 'Are you sure?' Seriously, she'd picked on the wrong one that night! For that I earned the nickname 'Terminator'. I laughed and didn't consider it a problem. I considered it part of my wild and rebellious nature, just one more thing I was willing to express in a way other people only wished to. *No one's ever going to push me around again,* I vowed.

Yes, I can hear myself and yes, the universe heard, too. There was a lot of learning in store for me.

In this world of equals and opposites something else started around that time. Days when, for no apparent reason, I'd jump on my moped and drive into the hills, guided as to where. The guidance was subtle: a tickle in my belly, constantly harangued by the loud voice in my head. Once my 'mystery teachers' realised what an awkward student I was, full of doubt and logic, they'd come up with the most amazing game plans to hoodwink me into innocent compliance. Back then I had to find *the* parking place under the steady beat of my head's, *What the fuck are you doing?* Then I'd walk into the woods. That was the next thing: it couldn't be any tree, it was always *the* tree, a *specific* tree, and not the same tree every time either. I had to wait until the feeling in my belly pacified the noise in my head, and then give it a hug.

Mostly things played out in my head. Not ranting thoughts or trying to puzzle things out though; more like my own private movie theatre, Monty Python-like random images, a show that I watched fascinated. Once there was a whole episode of the battle of dark versus light. I'd read that meditation can open you to other things; I was practising Transcendental Meditation twice a day. I always believed I'd opened a door when I took LSD at fifteen; I remember experiencing many such 'dreams' as a child. It had always been there, only lying dormant a long time then reawakening in Tenerife.

For the next decade without a physical teacher, not even a book, my inner guidance ushered me on a predestined path. I resisted it; *I didn't sign up for this!* I complained. It didn't matter; whatever I needed to learn was put under my nose like it or not.

There were some like-minded souls met along the way. Sometimes, when a few of us gathered on the beach or by the rocks, the conversation turned to the metaphysical. A young couple who also worked for Sun Sail told us about what they'd gotten into while living in the spiritual hotspot of Bath. I shared the tale of the warlock I met in London who taught me how to astral travel, and about some of my dreams, like flying over the highways of Chicago before I'd ever been. A few came to my place one night. Fifi and her brother were over on holiday, and the conversation went deep. We decided to try an experiment. I put my hands on the guy from Bath, planning to say whatever came into my head. All at once I started seeing things: flames, and a school. I said the names that appeared. Tears rolled down his cheek at the memories; he said I had seen so much of his past.

I was shaken by the depth of his emotions. Instantly I recognised the importance of this type of connection: we needed to know that there was something beyond the superficial and apparent randomness of life. It was the first time I had done anything quite like that since I was a kid. Well, apart from in Guernsey, that is; I'd put that down as a joke, a cry from the crazy women who tried to draw me into her world. Now though, in year two of my recovery, the intensity of this experience, so many dreams, precognitions, knowing when someone was going to call, I was really starting to wonder.

Little did I know how much more of that was to come.

All too soon the season ended. Bill, naturally—being so busy in South America—picked me up from the airport. Six weeks later he told me he loved me. A couple of weeks after that, he asked me if I wanted children.

I'd found my Bungalow Bill.

CHAPTER FOURTEEN

Motherhood, and the Toxic Tyranny of Trauma

Yes, life had run apace; it seemed that as soon as the magic words, 'Do you want children?' came out of Bill's mouth, we conceived, married, and moved to the country. That was late autumn 1993; our daughter Jessica was born six weeks early, January 1994. She was beautiful from the moment she arrived on this earth. Ill-equipped as I was to be a mother, I somehow managed to love and care for my tiny little daughter.

There are so many things life never prepares one for. Motherhood might be the most overwhelming, yet also the most transcendent. No one had ever prepared me for how wonderful, how profound and poignant, how miraculous this chapter in my life would be! There were days when motherhood knocked the wind out of me with heartbreak; there were other days when I saw the beauty in the mundane magic of everyday events, and found I could overcome my crushing heartbreak with a tender hug and kiss from my child.

Motherhood became my hard-won treasure—a powerful reminder to cherish each day.

The magical days of Jessica's growing up passed quickly. We drew, painted, created our own greeting cards, baked bread, learnt to cook, went on long walks, made up dances, stories and songs.

We were joined by a dog called Fudge, then a cat called Felix. Our house was always filled with shrieks of laughter and joy. When it was my turn to do the ballet run, Jessica and her friends piled into the therapy room, covering 'the client' with the multicoloured sarongs and throws that were left strewn around, then point candles at her, 'giving the purple light' or 'giving the green light' while making *serious sorceress*-type faces.

By the time she was six, Jessica frequently taught an aerobics class to anyone in the vicinity: adults, teenagers, children, age mattered not. I knew I had succeeded as a parent when a girlfriend of mine, Mel, left after our girly lunch thanking *Jessica* for her company.

Yes, by age nine, Jessica had far outgrown me in terms of social graces and diplomacy. It was obvious, it was true—and I couldn't have been happier.

With the arrival of Jessica in my life, I began a love affair with nature. Strolling naked on the sand, sun glistening on my hair, a cool ocean breeze caressing my skin. Standing in the freezing waters fresh from the hills. Hiking alone across deserted moors. Strong, fit and capable, a new passion stirred in my loins: not for man, not for any company; only for the wildness of the hills around me, awakened by the sunshine, fresh air, and the warmth of deep summer's earth.

As a child who had grown up during the 1960s, Mother Earth wisdom came naturally to me. I threw out the TV, cooked whole organic food from scratch, grew tomatoes and foraged for mushrooms. I honoured the earth, celebrated her cycles and even menstruated in time with the moon. Now a practitioner in NLP—neuro-linguistic programming—I modelled all that I did not know. I wrote lists and made schedules: *play with daughter, work on abs, start cooking.* My interest in fitness—having blossomed during university—turned, through a collection of chance circumstances, into a career as a personal trainer. My single-mindedness made motivation and staying power easy. I never skipped workouts. The fact that many of my clients did, baffled me: missing a session they'd arrive late the next week, slumping their shoulders in defeat. I felt like saying, 'What's your excuse this time? Dump that chocolate shake in the rubbish, lace up your trainers and hit the fuckin' gym!' The desire to combat this defeatist mindset led me to take a diploma in hypnotherapy, and soon yet another door opened on my horizon.

I dove in, converted my degree, wrote another dissertation and travelled to Manchester, Preston and Birmingham to pick up the rest of the pieces and become an accredited psychotherapist. Simultaneously I went deeper into the world of esoteric wisdom.

The guidance that had begun in Tenerife, with that divine intervention—that moment of spiritual rebirth, when I was on my knees in despair—did not stop there. Since that moment, my life went through such a catalogue of changes, inexplicable twists and turns, and unexpected outcomes that I believed them to be on a level more supernatural than ordinary. At times, I felt I had been lifted by the hair of my head by an invisible giant and placed on another path entirely.

I was not always willing; often I was kicking and screaming my objections.

Despite the universe's guidance, there was always a dichotomy, as if I was destined to play out life in two separate dimensions: the skyrocketing of my spiritual growth and esoteric awareness grew simultaneously with the emergence of a tantrum-filled emotional child. I had been in therapy since I started training as a psychotherapist in 1999. I embraced it fully, talking it out, crying for my inner child, cleansing my energy field, practising rituals of every kind. I thought I had come to terms with my childhood. I certainly recognised that I was no longer my past; it may have made me who I am, but I was growing to like that person. Yet I was continuously faced with my blocks. There seemed to be a parallel process between my successes and my shadow. This was not new—only this time, the stage wasn't modelling, or being Marilyn, or even my addiction.

The stage was my marriage.

* * *

Superficially Mr Nice Guy, I felt Bill showed his distaste and disappointment in me in a variety of ways: criticism, scoffing, unwillingness to participate or to open up. 'For fuck's sake, must you analyse the arse out of everything? I've been working all day and my stomach's playing up, leave me alone!' My mother-in-law flagged up the energy behind Bill's continual bitching and moaning and putting me down. She said that when guests were due to arrive for dinner, Bill would check the placement and cleanliness of the cutlery after she had laid the table. Those words echoed in my ear against a backdrop of Julia Roberts swimming the Atlantic in *Sleeping with the Enemy* when Bill called me out for slurping my soup, having a stain on my top, or being unable, as I learnt to cook, to keep the kitchen walls clean. *Arghhh!*

My early family life had been couthy. I'd been teased in a loving way about my lack of practical prowess, while acclaimed for my love of books and capacity in the classroom. So at first, Bill's jibes did not get to me so badly. *He's just a bit of a snob,* I told myself.

After one of our many fights I asked my father why I was the way I was, never being able, not even once, to give in to Bill on his terms. He replied simply: 'Wi' the life you've led, lass, you couldna be anything other than fiercely independent. You left 'e hoos at sixteen and made your ain wey in the world iver since. Of course, yer like 'at!'

Mum added: 'He canna master ye, that's fits adee wi' him.' Despite the love intended, I felt the constant, invasive pressure of their words. I understood them, I agreed with them, but they did nothing to lift the sadness of knowing I was living with a ticking time bomb. Whatever it was that Bill fell in love with, it was long gone.

The deepest cut was during countless dinners out. Having to watch my husband's face emote the fantasies in his head around whichever woman had the tiniest arse in the room devastated me. It did not matter how beautiful I looked—and I did look beautiful. I had matured into a stunning woman. I took care of myself more than I ever did when I was modelling. I was no longer bothered by the *not tall enough, not skinny enough, chocolate box enough* thoughts; My mind was calm, my body fit. I both looked and felt like *myself.*

And I liked her.

None of that seemed to matter to Bill. His standard was unachievable, a fantasy that existed only in his mind. How cruel Mother Nature could seem in a society that didn't hold space for our true selves, thereby discouraging respectful honesty between man and wife! If I ever spoke up—'What the fuck are you talking about now? Are you on your period or something?'—I would be risking a barrage of 'crazy bitch' abuse. When I raised the subject of an open marriage, Bill would bulge his eyes wide and say: 'What, we can shag whoever we want?' By his tone, I visualised him running about our small village like a dog with two cocks. Our philosophies were poles apart; he had no idea what I was talking about.

The resilience I had started to build slowly eroded, piece by tiny, little piece. He never allowed me to take the lead in bed, not ever. 'Ugly girls are better fucks!' he snapped, announcing that maybe I could lose some weight. In this way, his 'mind-fuckery' consistently reflected the lack I already felt within. In fact, I felt he met my uncertainty, insecurity and a longing for love with intolerance, hatred and rejection—yet kept insisting he did not want to leave, that I was a hopeless romantic, wanting more than life could offer. He didn't really love me in that way, and because of this, we should just get on with it, as that was all there was.

I found myself encaged in another prison: marriage. The irony was I had thought Bill was the prince who would anchor me to reality: safety, sanity, suburbia. When I met him, I felt so tiny, so small, so insignificant, so worthless, so wrong, so dirty deep inside. If only a 'normal' person like Bill would love me, I could learn to be different.

But it was blowing up in my face.

Eventually I got the message that my marriage was over. It was June 2004, at Brodgar's Ring in Orkney.

With me that night was an international group of Sekhem trainees. We were the largest group there and must have looked a mystical sight as we approached the stone circle on the first of three very special moons. As my group dispersed to explore, I spotted an enigmatic figure walking the circumference of the stones, spirit staff in hand. Inexplicably I felt drawn to him; a mere silhouette in the distance, he was somehow familiar. I watched his slow and deliberate progress from stone to stone; as he drew near, every cell in my body lit up and expanded to contain my whole consciousness in a single moment of time. I can't say I never thought I'd feel that way, ever experience such a moment, because I didn't know such moments even existed. Yet right there, right then I was aware of its exquisite nature. It was as if a different sun shone through me. It glowed from all around, from the inside and out—expanding, inverting through galaxies in light years and dimensions both known and unknown. All at once, I knew him: all he had ever been, all we had ever been, what we were now and our purpose, in a thousand sparkled imagines of lifetimes been and gone.

I was standing stunned, literally gawping when his lilting accent broke the spell:

'You had better see to your group.'

Shit! And off I scurried.

The following evening, huddled into the side of a megalith at the north of the Ring of Brodgar with Ashley, one of my trainees, I spied the approach of this same figure. ''Ere he comes now, I told ya!' Ashley whispered. I barely heard the beautifully polite hellos as the world shifted once more, and it was just the two of us.

'I have a gift for you,' he gently announced, with a knowing look that made my heart expand and my body melt in submission.

When I reached to take the clear quartz crystal from him, he clasped my hand in his, started stroking the back of my hand, and held that look, into the depths of my soul. My stomach twisted with delight. I met his gaze, and with it such love. I allowed myself to feel the moment, be in that space with all of me.

For a microsecond.

The next thing I knew I was a fourteen-year-old child again, bashful and gauche. I plucked my hand back and grabbed Ashley's: 'Let's all hold hands then, shall we?' Flushed with embarrassment, I tried to hide it, while humiliation burned at the back of my throat. *What a fool!* I hissed at myself. *So stupid! So awkward!*

We sat in the grass a while, then Ashley and I made our way back to the villa, where she said in her amazing Essex accent: 'You must be dead from the fucking neck down, girl! 'E's gorgeous, and 'e fancies the pants off you! Wot's wrong with you?!' I gulped, experiencing the heat in my groin. I had not wanted those feelings to go there. That amazing, spiritual love was not meant to descend to my base chakra—but with the help of Ashley, it surely did.

I retired to my room alone. I did some clearing and some grounding, walked around with my smudge stick demanding any darkness to be gone. I sat in the meditation pose in front of my altar with the statue of the goddess Sekhmet in the centre, candles either side of her as I begged for help: 'What does it mean? What should I do?' I picked up my tarot deck: 'Give me guidance, give me truth, show me the way!' I drew the Lover's card over and over—against phenomenal odds, I drew that card five times out of six draws. This told me one thing: I needed to go back to Brodgar. Make love to him in the far hill on the other side of the stone circle. That was what the voice told me. *Yikes!* my mind pleaded for amnesty. *Maybe I could just walk with him, holding his hand and see what happened ...* It was possible, the way it was between us, hardly any words had passed. Many years before, I had dreamt my daughter. I had also dreamt my future son. The way things were with Bill, the son was never going to happen. And somehow this young man was meant to be the father; I knew it clear as day. Spirit was offering me the boy with the moon and the stars on his head.

The whole next day I was racked with turmoil. I believed then—and still believe now—that if you have embarked on your personal sadhana, like it or not the teachings will come. Mine were surround sound technicolour movies that you could call prophetic dreams, hints that were more like hammer blows … and now a soulmate disguised as a thirty-three-year-old, extremely fit shaman.

The call is always to awaken, but there is also always a choice.

I felt trapped and unhappy in a marriage that I was terrified to leave. The irony being that here I was, high priestess from ancient times as it played out through the story of Sekhem, while on the earthly level I was lost, gone, scared, fumbling, unsure of myself. In the end, I bailed. I faffed around all day and then bailed. I will never know what glorious future lay down that path. Spirit had made an offer, and I had declined. I entered a period of darkness and spiritual torture. I chose between two men and had forgotten about myself.

The price for that was immense.

* * *

It took two years for the boil to burst.

Bill fell in love with a young Russian woman he'd met while working in Kazakhstan. I knew then my world had ended. The fighting was bitter and violent; we could not stand another four weeks like that, but Bill insisted he was returning home when he came back off rotation.

So, when in popped an invitation for a spiritual journey to Peru from a beautiful sister and fellow seeker, Maggie Erotokritou, asking me to come with, I grabbed the chance. Yet another of the many synchronicities that have blessed my life. Two days after Bill returned home, I walked out the door leaving everything I knew and loved. Twelve years of being a family, just the three of us, the animals, baking bread, weekend-long stay overs, outdoor pursuits and cosy fires. All over.

I was broken.

On the way to the airport, I stopped by the home of a dear friend. 'How can I do it, how can I leave?'

She put her arm around me and asked me to look at my feet. *My feet?* I did. 'Now,' she said, 'put one foot in front of the other.' I did. I walked forward with tears pouring from every part of my being.

Next thing I knew, I was in Cuzco chewing on coca leaves, and my soul was crying to the sound of the pan pipes. I continued to put one foot in front of the other until it was time to go home and start again.

* * *

In 2006, Jessica and I experienced the first of many non-traditional Christmases. The following spring equinox, I asked her to join me at the stone circle. She'd been very aware as a child; it was something I had helped her nurture. As we sat in the stone circle, I said to her, 'You know it's us now. I am going to be here for you, whatever happens. I'm going to be your mother and your father and we're going to be a family, you and me and the cat and the dog.' That was our pact, and limping and carrying broken hearts, we built a new life.

I muddled through, with both the help and hindrances from lovers and life's passers-through. My mum and dad were amazing: as Grandma and Grandpa, they were very much part of our family. Even once she had Alzheimer's, my mother always showed her deep affection for Jessica. Every Tuesday she would wait by the kitchen window for Jessica to appear at the top of the drive, watching her wave excitedly and run down the rest of the hill knowing that there would be Grandma's special mac 'n cheese waiting in the oven.

My parents stayed in my house so I could continue my spiritual tours to Egypt. We shared Sunday dinner at least every other week, so thanks to grandparents, pets and friends in between the crazy we did enjoy a lovely family life.

My sisters were not around much during that time. For many years, Kim continued to be there for me. Yet she had always found it difficult to share her own demons, and during this time I sensed she was slipping into her own personal hell—though she would never speak about it, and it's certainly not my story to share.

As for Lisa, I had to let go of any hope of healing that relationship. It seemed to me that the outward success Bill and I enjoyed when Lisa's own life was in an unhappy place sent her envy into overdrive. I made many attempts to bond with my sister, and there were times when she would move towards that, then push me away. I was the big sister, and I wanted it to be okay for my parents if nothing else, but Lisa's slaps were vicious, and I would be broken for three or four days after them. Bill found my tears unbearable; when he'd had enough of listening to it, he said: 'Your sister is a wanker, she'll never change, I don't know why you bother!' It was true: Lisa had displayed jealousy and distaste all her life towards me. She would not tell me what was wrong. I'd asked her on countless occasions, held out so many olive branches that were never taken. With all that I had come to understand I realised this was *her* path, not mine. I had to leave the turmoil and the toxic tyranny of trauma with her. It was one of the few times Bill had ever supported me, so I guessed that meant something.

There was one final episode, when as much as the rest of the family would have liked to continue to ignore her attempts to marginalise me, they had no choice but to acknowledge them. I somehow felt settled after that—sad but settled.

CHAPTER FIFTEEN

Sweet Surrender

Keeping our home in the Scottish countryside meant having a hard look at income. Luckily, I met a clever young man—another Bill, believe it or not, this one was Billy from Glasgow. Billy showed me how to apply the 80/20 rule, advised me hypnosis was the way to go. 'And you could use a bang-up website!' he said persuasively. Glasgow Billy looked more like a gangster than an entrepreneur; still, there was something about him. I liked Billy and I trusted him, took the leap of faith and within three months my clients had tripled, just as he'd promised.

Decision made, at the end of October 2006 I was seated on a British Airways flight, off to an advanced hypnosis training in London when the realisation hit: I needed to act in another department. The last few weeks had been crazy: my Bill was gone, and I was only weeks away from my fiftieth birthday. It probably wasn't a good idea to remain unsaddled for too long. I replayed recent events in my head … *Oh gosh, apart from that schoolboy gazing at my boobs as we stopped at the traffic lights on the way to the airport in Peru, not a single other male had given me a second glance that whole trip!* Okay, it was the last thing on my mind, and yes, it's all about the vibe, but I was accustomed to getting male attention whether I wanted it or not. Had I reached the 'invisible' age? Shit! That would be bad karma, losing a lifetime's ability to pull by the mere act of considering it just as he decides to trade me in for a younger model, waaaah!

Fuck that.

Oh my, I continued to myself. *Then you took Jessica for that week in Turkey, not even there amongst the hot-blooded Turks, nothing.* What was wrong with me? I flicked through the snaps on my phone—man, I looked hot, *really* hot. The divorce diet had rendered me buff with all those water-skiing muscles popping out from the newly shed unhappy layer. Even the hurt on my face showed a vulnerability that seemed quite attractive.

So, what was going on?

Going into therapist mode I remembered the story I'd heard about a well-known psychotherapist, thickly bespectacled, somewhat shy and lacking confidence with the opposite sex. Living in New York, he challenged himself to simply say 'hello' to female passers-by on his daily constitutional through Central Park. The 'research' was successful: many of the women responded. Emboldened, this New York headshrinker turned 'hello' into a chat, then a conversation, then a sly and juicy daily confession, graduating on and upward from there until in his own quiet way he earned himself a reputation as a charmer. In fact, at the ripe old age of eighty-three, he married for a third time—to a woman thirty years his junior!

Right, I thought, *it's time to get back on the horse. A master plan was afoot!*

* * *

The lucky and well-timed recipient of that thought showed up with eager lips and a fine Irish sausage the very next day.

Even more interesting was that from the idea's conception on that British Airways flight until I, for the first time in fourteen years, had sex with someone other than my husband, I had five new guys texting me. A mere twenty-four hours! That's what they call the law of attraction.

Danny Boy and I met on the training. I could see he got pipped at the post for a seat at my lunch table, so I let him catch me at the coffee break to get the chance to ask what I was doing that evening. I smiled. 'Sure, I got an upgrade with my Hilton Honours card, why don't we meet at the bar to enjoy the free hors d'oeuvres and wine, see you there at six?'

Danny and I had plenty to chat about. The evening passed well, and before we knew it, we were saying goodnight at the elevator. The kiss was pleasing, but no less so than the generous bulge in his trousers. I recognised the classic Mae West moment, and like the lady herself, I always appreciate it when a man makes it plain how he feels. I led the clearly tortured chap by the hand to my room; had he been sitting with that in his pants all evening? The situation was beyond words; his tongue was required elsewhere anyway. It was indeed the first to traverse the soft lines of my newly flattened tummy. I was coming before the tip of it made contact and the reassuring thrust of his thick, hard cock made me realise that life was indeed far from over.

Having a distant love affair allowed me to get on with other things, but now-and-again sex has never done it for me. So, although Danny and I became good friends, the relationship brought more frustrations than it solved, and it was time to look closer to home.

Chris, a local builder, had hired me years before as a personal trainer. He'd popped in to see about some work I needed done in the house. Over a coffee and catch-up about life in general—the whole village knew I was newly separated—he put in a good word for his plumber, Barry. Barry, originally from South London, did two-week stints for Chris, then enjoyed the next two weeks in the sun. Chris was keen to let me know he was neither a womaniser nor a gold digger, owned a house in Kent, a villa in Moraira and a motor cruiser. Chris clearly fancied himself as a bit of a matchmaker and was really selling this guy; after all, what better way to have him settle in the area full-time than hooking him up with a local lady?

Barry's version of the tale ran more like "The Three Little Pigs", with me being the third and lucky piggy who got the big bad wolf! Barry's sense of humour was one of the things I loved about him: he was quick-witted and had a knack for telling a tale. In that way, he reminded me of my father; I modelled a lot of my therapeutic and teaching tales and humour on those two men.

Barry was not my typical relationship. It was not love at first sight, nor was there any of that instant 'knowing'; my heart was still bruised. But we got there. He was tall and strong with blue eyes—well, usually red, white and blue as he would quip—handsome in his way and carrying enough of the bad boy with his South London accent and gangster-like countenance to be interesting. A romantic at heart, Barry proposed before we had even kissed. Six weeks later he had my name tattooed on his arse. He told me he had fallen in love during that first job when I'd had a classic damsel in distress moment.

The Sky engineer's protocol wasn't going to work with what the builders were doing. Overwhelmed and knowing it was a situation I was likely to handle badly, I followed Barry to his van, asking him to step in and organise the chaos. Having forced Bill to remove all our TV sets when we set up home, here I was just a year after we broke up, installing a fifty-inch mammoth right over the hearth and meeting my new man in the bargain. Jessica reported later that her dad had a hairy fit when he caught sight of it from across the field. I had to laugh.

Tattoos and proposals to one side, our romance started slowly. Barry was a drinker; specifically, a white wine drinker. After a bottle or two he'd call me up and tell me how he had been thinking of asking me out and wondering what my response would have been had he done so. It was cute, but it was only when Ben, his oldest son, came to live with Barry and they adopted a new puppy, Dougie, that my Jess fell in love with the beautiful picture of family life that portrayed. We both desperately wanted that, so I was not far behind her.

The following spring, I swept Jessica and Barry's youngest son, Dom, off to Florida for water-skiing, while Barry made massive renovations to the house. He was certainly a doer, and I loved the family life we constructed together. Scotland, Spain, the boat, occasionally Kent and sometimes quad bikes, BBQs, and mattresses in the back of the builder's van and off we'd go! A couple of bottles of Bud, a fish and chip supper, with Van Morrison's 'Into the Mystic' playing as we gazed out to the vastness of the ocean.

There were nine of us: Barry, Ben and his girl Jodie, Dom, Jessica and I, Teddy, our chocolate lab, Dougs and Felix, and as many of the four grandparents as were available. It was a good time for us: we were the family I'd always dreamt of. Eventually our problems overtook us, but still, we had made a great team for a while.

After the initial thrust of moving on with my life post-divorce, the burden of being a one-woman band, self-employed and never quite financially secure ended in sheer exhaustion. Bringing Jessica up with so many hindrances from her father was a huge part of it. Bill seethed with jealousy when he saw what Barry had done to the house. He hated that I was managing, blamed me for everything, and warned me that I owed him money when the reverse was true. He couldn't speak to me without shouting or making some snide remark when he was out of Jessica's earshot.

I'll never forget the icy hand that wrapped around my heart the day he said, 'Do you want pain? I'll spoon-feed it to you on a daily basis, if you like.' He did. Bill stood on me repeatedly until I finally grew strong. The evil of those days made it impossible for us ever to put on a joint front for Jessica's sake. I took each episode to heart, and it took me days to recover. Eventually I conceded to my father's advice and banned him from the house. It forced me to grow my businesses, as I would never let Bill win and see me downtrodden—it was enough that he had broken my heart. The result, however, was that I was full of nervous tension, on the ever-spinning hamster wheel. Life was like being a junky again, but without the euphoria.

Country life means needing to drive your kids everywhere until they can drive themselves. That means owning a four-by-four. I burned two clutches out on my Land Cruiser trying to reverse that bloody horsebox. I was hopeless. I managed to be Mum, therapist, housewife, but totally failed as horsebox driver and handyman—it took me five years to realise I was supposed to do something called 'home maintenance'. Being that I was worse than useless in that field, Barry's improvements in some ways left me with more problems than they solved. Mostly I was just tired; often I was stressed. The peace I had found during my early marriage had now become an endless round of doing, and my new drug was getting on with it. I didn't like it, not one bit. Additionally, Jessica and I were not getting on. I suppose the writing had been on the wall: my daughter had gone through hell in the last volatile years of her mum and dad's marriage and the first years of divorce. The court case with Bill was never-ending. I had put on weight, felt depressed, was drinking a glass of wine most nights, just really struggling.

As always, it was my sister Kim who awakened me to the brutal reality that it was time to change.

'You need to get your life back, Vicki! Jessica's sixteen now. Your divorce is over, it's time for you to start living again!' She was right, and I took it on board; it was time to wake up from the haze of hurt I'd become stuck in and open my eyes to life again, time to drop the doom and gloom, purge all my dysfunctional relationships, time to channel my inner bitch again.

Time to take action.

* * *

In May 2012 I signed up for a Tony Robbins event in London. Doing a fire-walk with six thousand people was tremendously empowering, Tony was amazing, and it was exactly the shot of spiritual adrenaline I needed.

Then on the summer solstice, I trekked to Inverness to participate in a vision-quest. During the preparation, it was explained that we needed to choose a sacred circle, nine meters in diameter, completely out of sight of everyone else but within earshot of base camp. That was to be our home for three days, the only communication a call-and-answer system for the drums. During the preceding days, we stocked up with water and, being Scotland, put up a tent with a sleeping bag and whatever clothing needed to stay warm. Finally, I carried up my diary, my pen and my drum.

The three-day fast opened with a ceremonial sweat lodge before we headed to our sacred space. I'd expected the hallucinations to begin when hunger kicked in; however, I was in an altered state straight from leaving the sweat lodge. I beheld visions of nature spirits from that very first night, and many things became clear to me during those three soul-searching days.

I went home, repacked and left for Turkey and a two-week yoga holiday. The fast followed by two weeks' hardcore vinyasa put my body back in shape. I was glowing when I met Kim in İçmeler for a week's rest and relaxation. I had also made up my mind: no more partners! 'I'm just going to have a toy boy from now on!'

Everyone had heard of Turkish toy boys; they had quite the reputation for being gigolos, so my eyes were open and my body on green for go. *A toy boy would suit me perfectly,* my brain reasoned. *My business was thriving, I could come here now and again, get fucked stupid, go home, and get on with my life.* It sounded like a logical move. And here we were, only one more thing to be done: handbag shopping!

Kim knew exactly the handbag she wanted before even leaving Scotland. She had discovered the place to go was the big market in Marmaris on the Wednesday. We decided to jump on the water taxi from İçmeler. It was glorious, feeling the warm sea air over naked arms and legs as we chugged over the waves. I was wearing a flimsy multicoloured maxi dress with my skimpy bikini bottoms, no bra, a huge floppy bright pink hat, and a pair of 'exercise your bum as you walk' platform sandals. A woman with some style, comfortable in her own sexuality but past caring about fashion alone. Okay, and maybe just slightly eccentric.

Chatting aimlessly, my sister and I strolled from the marina through the backstreets and into the market itself. It was the very first shop, brimming with handbags, belts and wallets. Time to get down to the serious business of shopping. The cheeky little salesman asked me if I had sheep. It took me a minute, then I realised: *Ah the hat! I'm Little Bo Peep!*

'Yes, I have fifty in my garden in Scotland.'

His smile was engaging, and he held my eyes easily in the twinkling brown depths of his. 'Oh, you've got a good luck charm,' he remarked, taking the Turkish eye of protection I wore above my left breast between his long, beautifully tanned fingers, his pinkie resting on my nipple as if it had always belonged there. Electrical shock waves shot throughout the whole of my body. My eyes opened in response, my lips parted, and my fanny regressed twenty years. With his hand on the small of my back he asked if I wanted this bag or that wallet; I have no idea what his exact words were. I was stunned, as shot after shot of testosterone and young pheromones blasted my senses like a tommy gun. He was irresistible: a combination of flashing strong teeth, soft lips, glancing touches and such an intense undercurrent that my feet floated towards the back of the shop. I had never wanted it this much. Before I could say anything, the words leapt from this man's tongue:

'I have to fuck you …'

'Yes, you do,' I replied.

He did. Sudden, raw, electric ecstasy without pause or thought.

Grinning, we stumbled out of the back shop. The next thing I knew I was laughing with my sister, who'd waited politely on the stool sipping the obligatory cup of chai as if I had disappeared to try on a dress. 'Fucking hell,' she chuckled, 'he came out and was like 'OH MY GOD!' as if he'd just gone ten rounds with Mike Tyson!'

Clearly, I had not lost my touch.

Plopping the pink hat back on my head, the salesman came out to say cheerio and ask me to dinner that night. I declined: 'We have to take the water taxi back to İçmeler now and I'm not coming back to Marmaris again.' Salesman to the bone, he was never going to take no for an answer. Eventually I surrendered and said, 'Yeah, okay, I'll meet you.' I had no intention of keeping the date. *This is just some young Turkish guy who shags everything with a heartbeat,* I told myself. *He may have another notch in his belt but so have I.* Kim and I strolled round the market; she found her handbag, I bought some cashew nuts and satisfied with our outing we climbed on the boat back to İçmeler.

The back shop bang was unintentional yet encouraging. I was serious about getting a toy boy—one with a little more permanence, though. 'I quite fancied that guy that put the little Turkish eye on me,' I confessed to Kim. 'He was more my age.' Handbag Guy was young, Turkish-Eye Guy in his mid-thirties. He had beautiful, long thick hair tied back in a ponytail and was probably more my style. 'Come on, let's go and see him!' We'd met a couple of days earlier, and it was looking like he was about to chat me up when a woman came along and interrupted.

The same happened that night. Just as we were moving towards his stall, a second blonde woman came about. So that was that. Turkish Eye Guy was clearly popular. A good sign though, so two nights later I said, 'I'm gonna go down there once more and see if I can get chatting.' Off we went, and for a third time some other woman was there first! *Humph.*

Determined to hang about and discover if there was something between us, I said to Kim: 'Let's get some cold drinks and then go back.'

As we exited the shop I suddenly heard my name—'Vicki, Vicki, Vicki!'—and there he was, jumping out of a car.

'Oh, what are you doing here, I thought you were in Marmaris!' I blurted out.

'My cousin has a stall here … but what happened to *you*?' He was mad at being stood up, clearly not used to it, and although he did rant on, it was spoken with good heart and charm. 'Come on, let's say hi to my cousin!' he announced with one eyebrow raised sexily. As we walked back through the now bustling stalls, I knew. What were the chances, but my hunch was strong and true: *Turkish Eye Guy was Handbag Guy's cousin!*

Handbag Guy was off to Turgutreis to set up the stall for the next day. 'I'll try to get tomorrow off,' he vowed, 'and we'll spend it together.' Intrigued, this time I did show up.

We met at the cousin's place. 'I want to fuck you properly,' he announced. 'Let's go and get a room.'

Understanding *I'd* have to pay for the room, I asked: 'Are you a gigolo?' He laughed, and there our relationship began.

There was a lot of fucking to be done before the talking started though. It had been a sadness in my life that I had not often experienced the beautiful lovemaking that a man and woman can share, yet I can honestly say I have been fucked well in my time. Yet this, thirty years my junior, a boy to me, was my 'Never mind I'll find someone like you' person—I'm dead certain about that because *he told me so.*

That's how I met Handsome Harry.

No one ever fucked me like Harry fucked me. And no one ever loved it so much. Harry could fuck six times a night—and I mean *six orgasms!* Whenever I was gasping for breath and needed to say, 'Fuckin' 'ell, you'll have to stop, that's enough!' Harry would give a gentlemanly sigh.

'Okay, okay, just give me a minute …,' he'd say and make this gorgeous sexual drone and just will himself to come—yes, on a sixth or a seventh time! Even as a teenager I'd never met guys who could do that! Nor was I ever raw. It was never too much, never rough with eyes screwed tight shut; it was hot and passionate, or gentle and slow, and we certainly had our share of deeper loving moments too, we really had it all.

The boy was a legend. I have never met a guy who laid so many other women—I guess Harry earned the experience somehow. His cousin's girlfriend told me she was once there for twenty-six days, and Harry had a different woman for twenty-four of those nights.

Virility was a national pride, according to Harry. The first winter we spent together, as we were unpacking the car outside our villa, I asked what the security guy was staring at. 'It's because he knows I am going to fuck you all night!' Harry grinned.

'How does he know that?'

'Because I'm Turkish, stupid!'

Women would gaze at Harry when we were out together, and Harry loved it. He was a beautiful young man—not only on the outside, either. He had a big heart and was honest even when he shouldn't have been. 'I don't lie, stupid, only the small bullshits that fall off my tongue,' Harry would say. Like telling me he was thirty every time he had a birthday—and he had two birthdays every year! I was fifty-six when we met; it turned out he was twenty-six back then.

That first night during rests we spoke. And we spoke. And we spoke. He asked: 'What did you mean when you said I was a gigolo?'

'When I was in London,' I told him, 'I used to play that game, too. I know exactly what you guys get up to. I think I could teach you a thing or two.' We laughed.

'Show me how you suck a cock then!'

Harry was a rough diamond. His eyes sparkled at the friendship we were forming; it was the beginning of a relationship that lasted three beautiful years. We became as close as any two people can be. There were no lies between us, only honesty. It turned out to be more of a love story than a toy boy tale: *The Gigolo and His Professional Bitch.*

The odd thing was, having been insecure most of my life, I never felt more secure than I did with Harry. Yet honesty had its limits, as I discovered when I recounted a date I'd been on in Scotland, and Harry flung himself on the bed pulling his chest hairs out in a frenzy until I reassured him, 'It was only dinner!' There was really nothing to hide: my dates at home were for the social aspect. For me being with Harry was a journey of growth that brought many blessings. I never told him what to do and listened to the tales of his conquests ... until one day they just stopped.

I recognised Harry was going through a metamorphosis; it would soon be time for him to settle down. Yet the fire between us never dwindled. 'I just love fucking you,' he confessed, and his actions left me in no doubt of that; we were just a good fucking fit.

We just *worked.*

* * *

When I tried to sweep the truth of my marriage under the carpet, the cosmos gifted me with divorce. When I felt tired and old, it gave me young love. I am amazed and grateful for its gifts every single day of my life.

My travels to Turkey delivered another gift: my first meeting with my dear friend Seda Shambhavi, my companion and confidant as I have tapped out many of the words of my story. Passionate travellers, and now in Goa, she and I had plenty to share as we walked along Putnam Beach, where we'd stop for freshly squeezed pineapple juice and a giggle at the old stoner who lay there frying on the sand with his psychedelic budgie smugglers and matching shades. Some days we'd take an early morning stroll through the forest. Others we'd visit Palolem with its amazing vegan eateries, stopping for lunch or to treat ourselves to a vegan Snickers cake, two forks and coffee. We ate our Christmas dinner on the beach, watching the Chinese lanterns carry wishes into the sky, all the while chatting aimlessly about life, love and our respective journeys. It had been a long two years since I'd been in Turkey; now we filled in the gaps with great gusto.

A fellow author, Seda and I worked on our own books during what we called 'office hours': a time of silence only interrupted by the ritual of passing the kettle from balcony to balcony of our little neighbouring bamboo huts, and the sounds of surf, passing trains, crickets, crows, dogs and laptop keys.

We decided on a trip to Hampi, sleeping in double bunks as the overnight bus rocked us in a steady rhythm into the region of Karnataka. Checked in, we delighted in finding Lavazza and Wi-Fi, five paces from our guest house amidst the typical hub-bub of life: cows, street food, playing children, backpackers and families going about their business. We moseyed that day away, strolling by the river watching the sacred bathing rituals, identifying the followers of Shiva garbed in white, Hindu pilgrims in that fabulous bright orange and those dressed up to the nines to pose with tourists like us.

It was then that Seda asked me: 'Why did you end it with Harry?'

Forcing a half-smile, I tried to give a breezy answer. Yet I knew Seda wielded her own sixth sense about Harry. Knowing my truth was safe with her, I pondered. 'I think I knew I'd had the best of it. It was time for Harry to settle down, and I wanted to remember it at its sweetest point.'

And the sweetest point it was!

Harry and I spent our last six weeks in a beautiful hotel on the coast of Antalya. We booked in as husband and wife, and I wore a wedding ring. No one cared that I was twice Harry's age or that I was foreign; we were married and treated like any other couple. It was over the Christmas holidays, and the hotel was full of couples there to enjoy the celebrations. I remember every morning going up to breakfast before him, just like all the other wives, setting his place at the table, getting his salad and herbs, ordering his omelette, and making his tea. Every woman did that for her man. I felt accepted by the other women. We'd say good morning to each other, how are you, and smile. They were shy in the beginning, but as they grew used to me, I felt a strong sense of belonging. I'm so glad for this experience: it was so out of my usual world and my beliefs. Before this experience, ignorantly I would have called their behaviour submissive; now I could see the warmth and love in it. During the Christmas and New Year's celebrations we had lots of other couples to talk to, and I learnt that life is never as straightforward as a single belief.

Harry and I fell into a routine of eating breakfast together. We'd go out for a coffee, maybe take a walk along the seafront. In the afternoon, he would go fishing off the rocks and I'd work on my laptop or write while watching him from the fifth-floor window. Sometimes I sat in the late afternoon sun nearby the rocks, with a bar of chocolate. I'd order us coffee, knowing Harry'd be up to join me before it arrived.

Every night we'd dress for dinner. Harry would want to know how his moustache looked. I'd ask if my bum looked big in my outfit—inevitably this led to delays and having to reapply my lipstick. Most nights we'd go to our favourite local eatery. Before we left the owner painstakingly helped us write out the 'secret family recipe' so I could make it back home.

Come Saturdays, we'd go upmarket to a BBQ-style restaurant, often with live music. Harry would drink a few beers and I would have a glass or two of wine. I only spoke basic Turkish, so the night I discovered one of the waiters was fluent in English, I smiled at him a lot, encouraging him to engage in conversation just to have someone else to talk to in English. That was when Harry went ballistic. He went to great pains to explain to me that the jacket draped over the back of the chair was *his* jacket, and no one else was allowed to look at *his* jacket, or speak to *his* jacket, or take *his* jacket, because it was *his*. It was the same for his bottle of beer: it was *his* bottle of beer, no one else should drink *his* beer or look at *his* beer or touch *his* beer.

Harry said it rather well, and it wasn't hard to take. He pointed out the attractive young woman at the next table—she couldn't keep her eyes off Harry. He explained that she wanted him to fuck her; he said it happened to him all the time, but she couldn't have him because *he was with me*. I knew this to be true: Harry had—and could have—more women than any other man I have ever known. Yet he never disrespected me when we were together.

That night, when I rose to ask where the toilet was, Harry leapt to his feet and led me there. It was downstairs; he stood outside the toilet door waiting, then escorted me back upstairs to my seat. He did that every time. I saw other men do that, too. Quite a different world, for me, and for a while, it was a paradise. Harry and I spent almost all our time together, easily and naturally, we only fought about silly things, like smelly feet (his) and too much work (mine).

After we said goodbye, and I'd returned to Scotland, Harry called me. 'I don't want you to come back.'

His ominous tone stunned me. 'Why would you say that? We had a wonderful time!'

'Every time you leave, I feel as if my arm or my leg has been cut off. So I don't want you to come back unless you come to stay.'

Well, that was that.

* * *

'*Mais je ne regrette rien*,' I said, giggling, and ordered more chai. At last, I had finished my story, and Seda, seated next to me, said: 'Only a really strong spirit would have designed such a karma that you have seen!'

I smiled at her wisdom.

Yes, I have been gifted with the people and experiences I needed. Earlier I called it 'training'; I meant it. So many of us think of training as physical exercise, as mental conditioning, as education or orientation or coaching, as the preparation we are drilled in, the tutoring we are schooled in, the certificates we may or may not frame and display on the walls.

But it is so much more.

Sometimes when you get far enough away you realise what your life has been.

Sitting in the Mango Tree in Hampi last night, sharing that last piece of my story, I wanted to cry for myself, and the battles my body has survived. Challenges were placed in my path, by people who wanted me in a way I did not want them, who were jealous or who somehow thought I owed them something. Mostly they were people I had cared for. Mostly they were challenges I gave myself—I know that. But my battles and challenges don't tell the whole story. The past is not reversible, but there are happy endings. Mine is one of them. I am content now. I have surrendered to the rhythm of living—the light and the dark, the cruel and the beautiful, trusting the power of love to uplift and sustain me. And while I will sleep in a simple dwelling tonight, today I only need to watch where I put my feet, hope Seda and I do not get hangry at the same time, that I don't drop my purse, lose my specs or forget what town we are in, as we watch the ever-fascinating kaleidoscope that is India, that is the world, that is the universe, that is *life.*

Afterword

When I was six years old, I was called a 'problem child'; at fifteen, 'a mental case'. In my sixties while writing my story, the awareness of what we now call 'neurodiversity' has seeped through. I can even claim it as a superpower.

I asked my mother: 'What happened when they told you I was a problem child?'

She said she had always wondered why I was different, that she'd said to my father: 'Fa's she like, fit will I dee with this quine, she's nae like onybody else.'

My father replied: 'She's jist Vicki.'

There never seemed to be any reason to speak of that rape, until that day it just fell out of my mouth. I tried the same word, *rape*, on a girlfriend from home: 'Oh come on, Vicki, it happened to all of us.' When I was fourteen, I thought like that too. When I was eighteen, before I had even heard the phrase 'objectification of women', there I was helping to build a myth as to what women are. It was a myth that bit me back several times, like building a Frankenstein that hides the real you, then wondering why no one can see you.

I see that same search on so many faces that come for my help as a therapist. Perhaps when they sit with me, and we laugh at our foibles, they can sense and feel inspired by the stillness I have found in myself, my desire for a better world and my love for all that is around me. I have all that safely tucked within the divine self, the part of me that can hold the energy of whore, priestess and goddess, even in a world that likes to both revere and belittle what it cannot understand. Yes, the world has hurt me; it will probably continue to hurt me. All I can do is be me as honestly and authentically as I can in the hope it will lessen such blows for children of the future. It has taken a lot of digging deep and peeling back to get here and somehow find peace in it. I am not sure that I would recommend it as a path. I hope our young people today can do better, and often wonder what models they need to determine their own path and somehow balance it all out. To create a future where authentic and honest collaboration allows us to grow beyond previous limits. Where we can have conversations without denial or blame, conversations that open and expand learnings. Safe spaces where mothers become enabled to hold and alchemise the depth of ancestral trauma. To thrill in the uniqueness of their children without the stress a rigid, unseeing society can bring.

Part of my journey will be continuing to do what I can to help others with their hidden stories. I feel that sharing my own is my contribution to the quiet revolution I sense growing in the world.

I have been blessed with a beautiful daughter, le plus beau-petit-fils, and a handful of very dear and beloved friends. I choose carefully who I spend time with. The rest of the time I walk in nature, tend to my garden, and tell my stories.

I hope you enjoyed this one.

About the Author Postscript

With Barry's renovations and my energy work, our Scottish home became—well, I am not sure I can say mine, but I am without doubt the caretaker—a quirky and intriguing Scottish village variation of a 'Laurel Canyon-type commune'. It has served as a retreat for many visitors including those on the path to self-discovery, environmental warriors, budding artists and writers. I am helped in this endeavour by woofers, workaways, karmic yogis and friends, many who have found it to be a life-changing experience. I am proud of my boho existence, of being a mum and healer at heart; in fact many woofers have left calling me the best Scottish or woofing mama ever.

Something that began out of financial necessity and the deep desire to allow Jessica to remain in the home she had always known and loved until it was time for her to spread her wings, became something I loved.

There were times during the summer months that the front room looked more like a laundry than a lounge. That was woofer season, and it was great having young people around the house again. The woofers had their own caravan, dubbed the 'Man Cave' by my dear friend and long-term woofer, Q. By the summer of 2017, this trend was in full force, and I had a very interesting household. Connor, the musical chairs lodger, who literally shifted to whichever room was empty. Graeme the ghillie who occupied the chalet in the garden that the gang had named 'Castle Grayskull', the place to go for pre-drinks. Ukulele-playing, dreadlock-wearing Paul who turned up from time to time and slept outside in his renovated furniture van. Elia who thought nothing of walking the sixteen miles into the next village on his day off with a raw cabbage in his hand for a snack. Niki, Coline, Anthony, Julia, Alex, so many beautiful people who enhanced my life, too many to list here. There were as many as ten around the kitchen table on some evenings; friends, family, residents, we would chat away fantastically. I never, ever planned it; it grew organically. The right people just gravitated here. Even through the big struggles I had during some of those years, these guys, my family of choice, were there for me. With their help I started taking Airbnb guests too. Then one day I looked up and thought, *Oh my, I have a commune!*

Still, the gypsy blood ran hot in my veins. I'd had a love affair with Egypt right up until the revolution. Harry and I travelled over much of Turkey together. He showed me around his homeland with great pride; we visited Pamukkale, Cappadocia, Izmir and Istanbul as well as visiting all the tourist resorts around Turkey's incredible coast by car, bus, gullet and even tandem! Encouraged by

Seda to revisit India, I went to participate in the childhood deconditioning course, Primal, at the Osho International Meditation Resort in Pune. From there I went to Goa then Kerala, discovering Varkala, which became my second home for many winters. I returned from that first trip feeling I had recaptured the spiritual essence of my true self.

The Osho Tantra course followed Osho Primal; this time I participated in Lesbos and that was where I became a sannyasin. What I'd found is that rare place where you touch a fellow soul upon the same plane. Where easy laughter and talk flows like the sand of the desert in the breeze and falls into different shapes and patterns, each with a new and enticing delight. Where understanding happens without explanation and the common goal is simply to be. This was how I lived until the pandemic changed life for us all.

My beloved father left his body at the end of 2019. My sisters insisted Mum went into care; without Dad to back me up, I watched in stunned silence from the sidelines. Confined and confused she suffered unbearably. At the mercy of Alzheimer's cruel hand, she just wanted to die. The toxic family dynamic that had been simmering under the surface for a lifetime exploded. I literally couldn't take a step. During the period between my parents' deaths, crippled with arthritis, I became reclusive, didn't travel, and sat with this book. Edited, ready for the bookshelves, like a watchful brooding hen, I sat.

Michelle, one of my closest friends and my right hand on this journey and I spoke many times of the book as every woman's journey. We wondered how many other girls were either undiagnosed or unheard, how many mothers unable to hold space so that their children could speak. Over lockdown, with another friend, Natalie, we started hosting women's circles online. This seedling of an idea eventually grew into a not-for-profit established to provide a sense of belonging and well-being for women in this increasingly volatile world. We have great plans for it going forward. Being able to host events free at the point of delivery was game-changing. All the pain, all the wounding, the downright crazy experiences suddenly had a purpose far beyond me. Even the fact that I seemed to have been deposited in the hills of Deeside 'against my will' was now starting to make sense.

Although I had fallen in love with the land during my 'spiritual training' and Jessica's growing up years, I still longed for sunshine, often missed the hustle, bustle and vivid life of London, the je ne sais quoi of the city. I was conflicted and couldn't understand why I didn't just move until Sharon Blackie's *If Women Rose Rooted* helped me make sense of it all. My heroine's journey to the outer world of glamour and fame. The lessons of addiction and recovery. The return to the land, the re-rooting to Mother Earth, the deep swathes of silence and home. By the time I read Sharon's words, I understood that the deep divine feminine was now within; I'd transitioned from mother to wild woman to grandmother and was now honoured to be holding space for my daughters.

Mum finally left her body on 27 April 2023. During her early days in the care home, she went through a stage of asking everyone who was it that was pregnant: 'Fa's pregnant? Is it your Jessie that's ha'in' a bairn?' At the time Jessica had no plans in that direction, no twinkle in her eye, no baby daddy, not even on the furthest horizon … Yet he must have been hiding in the wings, as my grandson, Albie, was born on 22 May 2023. My mother had known, and we like to think that she and Albie met on their respective journeys between the worlds.

I got my second hip replacement on 3 May 2023, and once more I can walk in the woods and swim in the waters of the River Dee and the roaring North Sea. The journey goes on. A journey that would not have been possible without the friends and colleagues who have helped me along the way and most of all my beloved parents who loved me unconditionally and taught me that it was special to be different no matter what.

* * *

I'd like to give special thanks to …

John Hartland, editor of *The Me I Want to Be*, who said: 'That's not a preface, that's a whole other book, one that needs to be written.'

My dear friend Robert Beedham, for all the signposting, support, the kicks up the arse I needed, and the coffees, calls and catch-ups throughout Scotland.

Sam Severn who, as developmental editor, helped me to take this book to the next level. I learnt so much from Sam, I will be forever grateful for his wit and gentle pushes. It was, however, a fair exchange as Sam, an American living in Nashville, can now swear perfectly in Doric thanks to me!

All the woofers and karmic yogis as mentioned above and all the many more who I don't have space to mention, yet nevertheless came and went from my life touching lightly on my heart.

The three beloved sannyasi who read my crumpled pages on the beaches of Lesbos and cried for my pain and the pain it touched within them.

Michelle with her super critique, super nannying, and super special 'Mrs Chelleness'.

Natalie who took the book from manuscript to social media posts and copy, cheering me on each step of the way.

Both Michelle and Natalie for gently pushing me along and then helping me hold space for the Story Club girls: Angela, Avril, Melanie and Jo Jo, whose feedback and responses as I narrated the book over the winter of 2022/23 helped my understanding to another level yet.

The first Well Woman Aboyne Groups who listened and shared and let me know how healing my story was for them.

Always and forever there for me, my mentor and friend Sue Washington.

My sweet Lahli without whose tears this book may never have been written in its current form.

And you, Jessica, who, despite my embarrassing Mum-ness, difficult personality and shameless potty mouth, told me—it's your story, Mum, and you should publish it.

I love and thank you all.

Vicki Rebecca is an accredited psychotherapist of 25 years, who runs a successful private Hypnosis and Neuro Linguistic Programming practice, including one to one, group coaching, and retreats all over the world to places like Egypt, India, Turkey, and the sacred sites of Scotland.

Vicki's harrowing past, quest for healing and transformation, as well as thirty-three years in recovery, has allowed her to become acutely aware of the hidden stories that hold us frozen in conflict. Through her ability to truly listen, hold space, create metaphors, and reframe client narratives, she is a beacon of hope and healing to those in suffering.

In "The Naked Truth: Diary of a Glamour Model", Vicki has shared her full uncensored truth to empower others to feel brave, release shame, and honour every part of themselves.

If you are ready to experience your own transformation, release shame, heal from your story, embody your own truth, and do this life changing work yourself, Vicki invites you to access "The Me I Want to Be".

Vicki published 'The Me I Want to Be: Simple Shifts to Authentic Wellbeing' in 2016, to teach the core learnings from her recovery and transformation to all the clients and students she'd worked with over the previous 20 years. 'The Me I Want to Be' fuses hypnosis, Neuro Linguistic Programming, meditation, and ancient Egyptian wisdom to transform lives through true authenticity and fulfilment. In many ways, it is the culmination of Vicki's journey, as well as having been the catalyst for Naked Truth.

The Me I Want to Be pack comes with The Me I Want to Be ebook; the instructional ebook and 19 MP3s amounting to over 10 hours of exercises, meditations and deep relaxations that will show you, exactly, how to be, The Me I Want to Be. Recorded by Vicki, for you, with love.

Normally £39.95, this special offer is exclusive for readers of The Naked Truth… £9.99 Get it here:
www.vickirebecca.com/reader